To Richard and Valentina

[signature]

D1452646

TESSA

MY LIFE IN ATHLETICS

TESSA

MY LIFE IN ATHLETICS

with Leon Hickman

WILLOW BOOKS
Collins
8 Grafton Street, London
1986

Willow Books
William Collins Sons & Co Ltd
London · Glasgow · Sydney
Auckland · Toronto · Johannesburg

Sanderson, Tessa
My life in athletics.
1. Sanderson, Tessa   2. Javelin Throwing
—Great Britain—Biography
I. Title   II. Hickman, Leon
796.4'35   GV1094.53

ISBN 0 00 218211 4

Photoset in Times

Made and printed in Great Britain by
Billing & Sons Ltd, Worcester

Contents

Acknowledgements

For their unfailing faith and kindness, I wish to thank especially my coaches Wilf Paish, Miklos Nemeth and Brian Newman. In years to come when Gladys Knight's version of *The Way We Were* brings memories drifting back, I shall think warm thoughts of the three of them: Brian who never lost confidence in me from the earliest days, Wilf for the Olympic years and Miklos in Hungary for giving me the sharp edge. There are dozens, maybe hundreds, of others who helped, too. I must, however, mention the Shrouder and DuCass families, my Aunty Kitty whom I once lost but found again, Clement Procope whose love I treasure, and Leon Hickman for putting my life story into words.

To Mum, Dad, my brothers and sister and our whole family, I like the way we are.

And to athletics, competitors and officials – how lucky we are.

CHAPTER ONE

Jamaica Farewell

'I hope whoever opens this Bible and finds this message will not destroy it. We are the Sanderson family. I have been here for quite a while and I pray that God will bless us wherever we go. I, Tessa, hope and pray that I may become an Olympic gold medallist, so whoever finds this letter you may say "God bless us".'

Tessa, 15 July, 1970.

I was 15 at the time I wrote this note in the untidy, preoccupied hand of a dreamer of dreams; a slender, bright-eyed schoolgirl scarcely aware of the joy, pain, laughter and anxiety that my search for the most coveted award in sport would bring. I took the piece of paper, apparently ripped from a school exercise book, and placed it in the family Bible, adding on the front of the envelope: 'To whoever finds this after we have left: enter', and on the back 'GOOD LUCK, Tessa'. Allow me, then, to take you forward a few years, in order, strangely enough, to give perspective to the days when carefree innocence became tremulous fear of the unknown ...

I love to laugh, letting my whole self go totally in a West Indian body-shaker. If I had to guess why I am often to be found where the chuckles are loudest, where the boys are cheekiest and the company enjoys fun, I would look for the answer in my upbringing in St Elizabeth, Jamaica. You need a pretty detailed map to find St Elizabeth and a sturdy vehicle to reach it up a potholed, car's-width track into the mountains where a dust storm swirls behind and the pitted surface bounces passengers about as if they were on a fairground ride. I went there in 1978 with a BBC team who had the brilliant idea – brilliant for us, anyway – of taking Sonia Lannaman, Sharon Colyear and me to Jamaica to film us back at our 'roots'. To be truthful, there weren't many that we could remember and when I approached St Elizabeth on that hot and worn old highway into the Blue Mountains, I was more struck by the wild assortment of trees than by any memories of my roots.

Half a mile from the village itself reporter James Fox, photographer Tony Duffy and I had to abandon our hired car and walk through the peanut farms into the mango trees and coconut palms among which a few houses, built by their inhabitants of thatch over whatever material was conveniently to hand, made up the little, friendly community whose people were gathered to greet me, the returning heroine. If this was my home until I was eight, and there was no doubt about it, I didn't recognise a thing, not even my grandmother from whom I had been torn in such distress 16 years earlier. Shame on me: among all the happy and quizzical faces, assembled to meet the girl who was hoping to win a Commonwealth gold medal a month or so later, Gran was just another smile until she was pointed out to me. Then, of course, they all came back, the memories of my guardian in those early years when I roamed, with increasing bravado, the richly-covered hillsides, climbed trees and played peek-a-boo barefoot through what I realised in 1978 was very nearly a shanty town. Such things don't matter to kids so long as they are happy and I know that I was happier and luckier than 90 per cent of the children I see around today. After a good cry and big hugs all round, I was treated like Royalty as the most famous daughter of St Elizabeth. In the emotional warmth of this community, which is really one big, inquisitive family, I was soon reminiscing about the days when I ran free or attended church in my best white dress and even one of the pairs of shoes that my parents sent me from that distant land where the Queen lived, England. Gran served up fried fish, bammy and banana and recalled with me the last days when the pure bliss drew to an end for a girl in pigtails and her older sister, Pat, then ten.

A few months before I was born, my father had left Jamaica in the earliest emigrant tide of the mid-1950s, quickly finding a job as a sheet metal worker at Ductile Steels, Wednesfield, close to the home that he and my mother settled into when she joined him just over a year later. Mum went to work at George Carter Pressing, also in the industrial Black Country belt that would later look like a hell-hole to a scrawny country girl who had loved the strong, clear light of the sub-tropical Caribbean. After my first brother Danny was born they saved enough to send for their two girls, Petronia, nicknamed Pat, who did not mind too much leaving our beloved home and Theresa Ione, who most certainly did. She showed it by dashing into the hills and hiding in a marl-hole until a search party collected her for the flight she would take from Montego Bay the next day. Gran tried to cheer me up by reminding me that I had planted a June plum stone so that the tree would always be a link with my first home. The tree now swamps the house but my sweet Gran would not let anyone touch it. I shall always be close to that lady who died three years ago and to the village where grown-up men and women remember me as a laughing child. Mind you, had I stayed there's no doubt I would have had three or four children of my own by now and a life working from dawn to dusk in the peanut fields. I love children but I prefer the idea that I can have them when I choose.

My first real memory of Jamaica was the day I actually left it with my sister Pat in the early spring of 1965. I still feel for that perplexed, weepy girl dressed to the nines in white bonnet, white crinoline dress and white shoes. We cried it seemed for the whole 14 hours of the journey, wondering with awe and fear what kind of life we were going to, knowing that nothing could be better than those carefree days in St Elizabeth. I sometimes wonder whether that uprooting has not given me a sense of insecurity about the future, and I would never wish such an experience on anyone. Pat was a bit luckier, she had an idea of who Mum was and even an inkling about Dad. To me, they were just two people who wrote to Gran and cared enough to send us shoes and clothes and presents. But I must say this, Jamaican families are usually very, very close and, however much prejudiced people like to label us as Rastafarians, muggers or ne'er-do-wells, most of us have a far stricter, more traditional 'English' upbringing of love and discipline than the average white family provides in Britain. Among my friends, I hardly know a black boy or girl who doesn't have sound values and loyalty. If you want to find the perfect English gentleman, you need look no further than Phil Brown, Donovan Reid, Aston Moore or Keith Connor, and for the English Rose, or rather orchid, Sonia Lannaman, Sharon Colyear, Wendy Hoyte or Shirley Thomas.

Many of these people were similarly brought over from step-families into the chill hostility of industrial England. I now realise I was one of the more fortunate ones, leaving Jamaica while still relatively young, joining my parents who could provide me with a good working-class home and, most of all, living in Wood End Road in Wednesfield which has no coconut palms but retains a friendly, village atmosphere where everyone knows everyone else's business. We were also fortunate because there was a rarity value in being black: only two families in our road came from the West Indies, the Morrises and the Sandersons. The later influx created problems for both black and white that remain to be solved.

At the time, of course, this was all before me and I can only say that the terror of landing in Manchester on a dark morning of sleet and then being shoved, like two small, sobbing packages, into a cupboard-like place to await collection remains with me to this day. Eventually, the eternal wait ended and suddenly Mum and Dad were there with kisses and hugs and kind words of welcome. It was a family reunion, fantastic, weird and solemn, as though Pat and I had been saved by someone and didn't know who they were or what was in store for us.

My memory then is of the cold, of the chimney pots and black smoke which impressed me during the two-hour drive to my new home. And there closes the vivid recollection, the film-like replay of a day of apprehension and loneliness that ended in the wonderment of a new family, including my three-year-old brother Danny, and Eric, one, British-born, who surprised me soon afterwards by rolling in white stuff called snow that fell from the sky. Even the beautiful, high Blue Mountains never had such a marvel. There were white people everywhere and they appeared not to speak the same language as me because I couldn't understand their Black Country dialect and they had no idea what my Jamaican *patois*, a kind of pidgin-English, was all about.

4

My parents had grown very refined, I could only assume, by their years in England. All those 'Good Mornings' and 'pleases' and 'thank yous' seemed unnecessary to a girl who had been able to grab fruit from the nearest tree without a word of fuss. As for fish and chips, when I was introduced to them I thought they were pathetic, lacking the taste or spice of a good old Jamaican country dish such as rice, peas and curried chicken. Today, I could be a fish-and-chip addict – I love them especially with lots of vinegar – a sure sign that I am as much British as West Indian.

The next obstacle was junior school, Wood End Primary, to which I was dragged in tears, like any other bewildered young first-timer. Once I had discovered the similarities between this and my previous school, I was much more at home especially as I was quite useful on sports day where egg-and-spoon, sack and three-legged races were just as popular as they were 6,000 miles away, the colonial heritage remaining strong in those Caribbean islands so far from my new home. Children of junior-school age are totally unaware of colour, or at least of any bias towards black, brown, yellow or white, so any fights I had, and there were a few, happened purely out of temper. The chief discovery I made before failing to pass my 11-plus was that I liked English lessons but not mathematics which I thought should be abolished for giving too much pain! Although most of the teachers at Wood End were fairly gentle and some even kindly, there was one who was not only unsympathetic but positively enjoyed rapping children with a ruler. She dealt with me in this way many times but although the punishment was often unjust it helped me stand on my own two feet. How I hated her! And in me, as in many a child, there formed the germ of a resolution that one day I would be able to say to people like her 'I have made something of my life and I haven't had to be cruel to do it'. Anyway, I was soon to leave her behind and in the autumn of 1967 to join the intake of Wards Bridge High, a secondary school for girls who regarded the scholarship set at Wednesfield High as clever-dicks.

I am told I was a lively, stubborn child who laughed a lot and was spoiled – this is according to my Aunty Kitty who came from Kingston, Jamaica, to live with us only three weeks after my move

– by my father, and my mother, Murphy. Outdoors I was a different person to the girl my family claims deliberately used to make a mess of lighting the fire, cooking or washing the pans. While my cunning worked with Mum and Dad, it had no effect on Kitty who watched this little monkey with a keen eye for the tricks of the getting-away-with-it trade. She disciplined me in a kindly but unbending way that once had me cooking half the night till the food was edible. Then it was escape – escape to the exciting world of the road or the playing field where I could challenge the boys at football, cricket and running. You name the game, I tried it. Home again, I discovered the kids' gourmet diet of beans. Mountains of them: on toast, on bread, by themselves, with egg, with chips; as long as they were beans in tomato sauce, I was in my true kingdom of indigestible delights.

My destiny was awaiting me but first the reality of prejudice intruded in ways that have left a permanent impression on me as they have on thousands of other black people. While bullying comes naturally to a few children, for the most part bad behaviour results from conditions at home, and particularly from apeing parents who have low standards. Within days of starting my new school one white boy, and I can still remember his name, called me all sorts of names and spat on my brand new uniform. I was so upset that Pat searched him out and gave him a thoroughly good hiding. She always was the tough one. Our parents weren't at all well off so you can imagine how upset I was on another occasion when a girl refused to return a pair of training shoes I had lent her. I said: 'Bring them tomorrow because if you don't and Mum finds out I'll get a real whacking'. The end of the week arrived and so I asked where they were. I couldn't believe it when she shouted: 'Shut up you nigger, coon! You black wog!'. They were my shoes and here was this girl calling me all these names. I exploded and in indignation started to fight. After school the struggle continued, but I never had those shoes back.

After a while, I became more careful about friends. One of them, Suzanne Kelly, joked about my name, Theresa Ione: Theresa as a result of an impulsive change of mind by my father who wrote to

Mum in Jamaica that she should abandon their original choice, Dawn, in favour of his sister's name which I share, of course, with the woman I most admire, Mother Teresa; Ione because, like Theresa, it has a lovely religious ring to it, and my family are Methodists and great church-goers. 'Two-ton Tessie' was Suzanne's answer to all this, especially as I was a skinny bit of goods. The name stuck so firmly that everyone took it up, even Mum and Dad, although for some while when he wished to sound highfalutin', Dad would pronounce Theresa precisely.

In Jamaica, I went to church on Sunday mornings and Sunday School in the afternoons and continued the practice of dressing up in my best clothes and attending the Methodist service in Wednesfield, along with men in the smartest suits and ladies in flowery dresses and fancy hats, until I was 14. I continue to believe faithfully in God, the God who helps you appreciate life a little more, who helps you care for other people and enables you to forgive others. I was very surprised when Mary Peters told me that she did not believe in God. She is such a good person that her atheism seems impossible to me, although I am sure that her treatment of other people owes a good deal to Christian teaching.

I once read of a boxer who called his autobiography *Someone Up There Likes Me*. That's exactly how I feel, not only because of the prayer I uttered to myself on the Los Angeles run-up but because of many little signs, one to my boyfriend, Clement, who stayed in Leeds during the Olympic Games and decided on the spur of the moment to go to a church to ask God to help me, whether I won or not. Clement was very frustrated when he found, first of all, that the door of our church was closed because it was a Saturday, and then that the next place he tried wasn't a church at all. Suddenly there were flashes of lightning and something inside him said that everything would be all right now. How do you explain that? It might be coincidence, and you could accuse us of being superstitious, but I prefer to believe that God was at work. I feel certain that had I come home empty-handed I would have been satisfied that I had done my best. I think everyone should make time to go to church, to find peace and serenity.

Academic education was never important to me, I just wasn't strong-minded enough. It was easy to excuse myself by rationalising that study was a waste of time when I knew that shorthand and typing would be enough to provide me with a secretarial career. I liked having fun and would not be persuaded later on that I could have a future as a physical education teacher if only I would work a little harder. Increasingly, however, I was attracted by various sports, and not just athletics in which I had first triumphed at primary school by winning the three-legged race with a now-forgotten partner. There was netball and hockey, too, and at about 12 I began to try the long-jump, high-jump and sprints. I even had a go at throwing the javelin but I was so bad, I tossed it away with the comment that it was a silly sport for a girl, anyway. Little did I know.

CHAPTER TWO

First Successes

Noreen Morgan, wherever she is now, may like to know that she was the initial reason for my interest in the javelin. I was able to beat the other girls in my year at just about everything but Noreen, known as Nogin, infuriatingly could throw the school's bamboo pole furthest, flying it with a rattle in the end across our playing field. This was too much for me and one day, I suppose I was 12 at the time, I challenged her to a special contest and was as surprised as she was when I won. Practising with this old javelin was as good a way as any to while away the lunch-hour and soon I had entered the event for my house on sports day, breaking the school record.

Two women began to take an increasing interest in my abilities, although it is true to say that I was not easily persuaded that training was necessary to improve. Most teenage girls would much rather giggle and gossip together or dream than work hard physically, especially if winning prizes for running fast or jumping high comes as naturally to them as breathing. Barbara Richards, the head of Wards Bridge High physical education department, would not let go, though. She was almost a pest sometimes when she forced me to push myself, and I wasn't very happy either when she put my name down for the Staffordshire county championships on 6 June at Aldersley Stadium, which is on the outskirts of Wolverhampton. At one stage our relationship was so difficult she threatened me with detention if I did not compete. Yet on the other hand, mixed-up little girl that I was, I once sat on the windowsill at home threatening to jump if my parents did not let me go out to train. That is where Aunty Kitty proved to be one in a million. She advised me quietly and stood up for me in some furious rows because Dad and Mum thought athletics were a waste of time. She's a crafty one, is Kitty.

9

She would wait until my parents were out and then send me off to train. When they came home there would be long arguments because they could not understand that I was not the academic type and that sport was very important to me. I often stay with Kitty now that she has moved to London – she's the next best aunt to Daley Thompson's Aunty Doreen, and how we laugh when she tells me what a snotty-nosed kid I was. No, she did not think I would be an Olympic athlete. She pinches herself each time I appear on television (and still tells me off when she feels I have strayed from her standards).

Barbara Richards was a more positive influence and I suspect she had a fair idea of the scope of my talent from the way she taught me not only to throw the javelin but to hurdle, long-jump and high-jump as well. Her encouragement and attention to the details of training were terrific for me, so much so that at those county championships, I won the javelin for juniors with a throw of 29.07 metres and came second in the high-jump with 1.47 metres. I was proud to be chosen for the English Schools championships, although I would have liked to have travelled further than Solihull, 25 miles from home, to show what I could do. These games are like no others, a lovely party where excited kids try to contain their drumming hearts behind an exterior of 'I'm not new to this, you know', where competitors are momentarily lost amid mild panic and teachers try to maintain control without spoiling the day. I wanted to win so badly, it was my last year as a junior, and how disappointed I was to come only third even if it was with the longest throw of my life, 31.86 metres. I have been told since that among the hundreds of competitors were Steve Ovett, Chris Boxer, Chris Benning, David Ottley, Charlie Spedding, Andrea Lynch, Gladys Taylor, Donna Murray, Mary Stewart, and my friends Sharon Colyear and Sonia Lannaman. Not a bad class, was it? Seven future Olympic medallists, counting myself. You can see why the 'English Schools' are vital to our athletics structure as the nursery of champions.

By 1970, however, I was beginning to realise that coming third wasn't in my nature. Coming first was and, being black, 150 per cent effort was necessary to make people realise that I had a cause. My parents were well aware of it and I think that is why they were so inflexible about academic qualifications. Solihull was bad, Crystal Palace the next year was to make me mad. Before my first journey to South London, however, I had to overcome my parents' objections and continue the routine that Mrs Richards had established. I also needed the basic equipment which, in one case, was a pair of tracksuit trousers, the acquisition of which proved to me that my mother, however she might huff and puff, was at heart on my side. One night I was watching from behind the half-open door when she sneaked on tiptoe towards my snoozing father, who had been on night shift, and pinched the money out of his pocket. I half suspect that Dad knew it was happening, too, and perhaps the charade was to show me that I musn't ask for money just for a fad.

Not long ago I went to a school in Walsall where most of the children are black. We were talking about starting in athletics when a lad said to me: 'It's all right for you, Miss. You had it easy, you were given everything'. I froze. I was ice-cold with anger when I replied: 'My first pair of spikes I borrowed from Maureen Tranter at Aldersley. My first tracksuit was second-hand, tatty and grey and I had to wear it for competitions. Yes, I had it all, didn't I?'. He stood there with his mouth open, then replied: 'I thought you were rich, Miss'. A lot of black children are down-rated because they down-rate themselves. I tell them they have to go out and graft for what they want, no matter what the consequences are. I don't know whether everyone would agree with that philosophy. I was an over-determined kid because I had an instinct that everything I touched I could do well at. In a way it was as if I didn't belong in my family because there seemed no source there for this relentless determination. I wanted at 15 to strive forward without let or hindrance.

That is why I was so upset when I was passed over in favour of Janeen Williams for the Staffordshire place in the javelin at Crystal Palace in 1971. I had not done very well the year before and my early efforts amounted to 38.44 metres at the furthest so perhaps being selected only for the intermediate long-jump should not have been such a surprise. I was eighth in the long-jump, reaching 5.31 metres which was below my best at the time. I watched the javelin all the while, knowing that I could beat any of the other girls and determined that there would be another time when I proved to the county selectors that their blindness had cost them and me a gold medal. The chance came quickly and how I revelled in it. What is more, I was able to throw in front of my friends and family when the WAAA intermediate championship was held at Aldersley.

After Moscow, there were whispers that I did not have the temperament for the big occasion, despite a record that included the Commonwealth gold medal and second place in the European championships. I knew differently and, indeed, those who have coached me – John Moogan, Wilf Paish and Brian Newman – contend that I am enough of an actress to turn on the big performance at the most appropriate time. The first evidence of this came on that beautiful day, 31 July it was, in Wolverhampton, when my longest attempt beat everything the others could throw at me, beat the meeting record and placed me 16th among UK seniors that year. Anne Goodlad had been favourite to win and her 40.62 metres was closest to my 41.72. I looked down the list of positions with particular interest because we had all been likely victims for a psychological trick when, as I opened the door of the changing-room, someone shouted 'There's Sue James, she's been doing ever so well'. At our age then this silly kind of claim – or perhaps little boasts along the lines of how new your shoes were or what a good coach you had – were about as far as the so-called 'psyching' went. In this case I had never heard of the girl and I thought 'Who's this? I'll have to be ruthless today'. I suppose it made me nervous but only in the right way, tense and concentrating on the job I had to do. Second throw, the javelin went perfectly and I let Sue James, Janeen Williams and Anne Goodlad know what I thought by doing a somersault there and then. That was the best piece of 'psyching' of all, though it wasn't meant that way. Ask Daley Thompson.

Other events were beginning to attract me by this time. A week after my 15th birthday, I long-jumped 5.36 metres indoors at RAF Cosford a few miles from my home and soon afterwards at Oldbury, in the heart of the Black Country, I completed my first championship pentathlon, winning the Midlands intermediate class with 3,590 points made up of a 5.41-metre wind-assisted long-jump, 1.56-metre high-jump, 28.4-second 200 metres, 14.4-second 80-metres hurdles and 8.16-metre shot-putt. With the exception of the javelin omission at Crystal Palace, it was a fine year for me because I won Midland intermediate titles in long-jump and javelin and came third in the WAAA intermediate pentathlon, scoring 14 more points than in Oldbury despite my worst long-jump (4.94 metres) for years.

I was not to make my choice between the javelin and pentathlon for a year and the factor that swayed it was, quite simply, my longing to travel. That first trip to Crystal Palace, albeit second class in the grubby compartment of an inter-city train, had inspired dreams of wonderful trips abroad, maybe because St Elizabeth was always in my mind, taunting me with its happy-go-lucky lifestyle. I worked out that it could be years before I was good enough to make the British team as an all-round athlete and, anyway, my older friends told me that there were nowhere near as many international vests to be won in multi-discipline as in specialisation.

Throughout my school life, it had been easy to dismiss other attractions – boys, discos and suchlike – but it was to be different after I left the direct influence of Mrs Richards, who had always seemed to be available when I needed to train. Anticipating the dangers, she decided that I should join Wolverhampton and Bilston AC and duly took me along to Aldersley where the club had acquired such an excellent reputation for bringing along young athletes. It was her insurance, she hoped, against me falling by the wayside and although eventually it was successful there were girls from school, Nogin, who inspired me to take up the javelin, and a very good runner, Joyce Bellwood, to name but two, who faded out for common reasons. I was to find others to replace them as close friends but not before I almost slipped away to become another minor statistic in local athletics. Usually it is a boyfriend, sarcastic jokes, a groundless fear of becoming unfeminine or just plain laziness – sometimes a combination of these – that ends a girl's athletics career before she has the maturity to make critical decisions. How often have you heard mothers or women at work say: 'I was rather a good athlete as a child but I stopped. Can't remember why now. Funny'. It is a frightening lament of lost opportunity but at one point I was so near to joining the chorus that I smile with relief at the thought of it. The things that saved me, I think, were natural talent and natural pride. I am not bragging, it just happens to be true that the gifts were born with me, as other gifts, some of them more valuable, are born with other people. When you are young, however, gifts are wasted and thrown away with hardly a second's thought and it was only the patience of a number of people who gave me lifts to Aldersley, especially the Walker family from Pool Hayes, or who paid special attention to my needs, that prevented me from an early dumping on the scrapheap.

The greatest drawback to training was the cold. If I live here for the rest of my life I shall never get used to the chill that settles on your skin and crawls deeper. It is bad enough now, but at least I can wear layers of tracksuits and thermal clothes. In those days, or rather those cold nights when the floodlights picked out the thin, freezing curtain of mist, I couldn't afford more than one tracksuit although I muffled up with other clothes. Mrs Richards took me to the stadium and introduced me to John Moogan, a schoolteacher, whose results coaching young javelin-throwers had begun to impress national officials. John emphasised that I was expected to travel to Aldersley three times a week, an amazing number of times for a girl who had become WAAA intermediate champion without having to resort to such strenuous work. I thought 'I can't handle this. There's all the time in the world to practise later'. Quite how I overcame this I don't know, except that, looking back, perhaps I had an in-built warning system.

My unwillingness to come to terms with the effort necessary to compete in such a technically difficult event surfaced in my new desire to be a track athlete. Running and hurdling did not involve weights – all the club required of me was that I should turn up on the day and do my best, which was good enough to earn me a place in the sprints and 4×400 relay team. It did not dawn on me at the time that had I been an East German I would have been a pentathlete (five events) or a heptathlete (the seven-event replacement) and possibly a challenger to Mary Peters before I was out of my teens. By the end of 1972 my best marks were: 100 metres: 12.3; 200 metres: 25.6; 400 metres: 57.3; 100 metres hurdles: 15.6; high-jump: 1.61 metres; long-jump: 5.65 (wind-assisted); shot: 9.92 metres; javelin: 43.06 metres. Don't think I am advocating the East German system, by the way – how could an individualist like me accept the unbending system of Communist Bloc countries? They never seem to laugh! On the other hand, coaches for throwing events were very scarce and if John had not been around, I haven't the faintest idea how I would have coped.

It was at about this time that I first met Brian Newman, who became my weights coach and a confidant on whom I can always rely for advice. I was frightened, like many young girls today, that he would turn me into a pocket-sized Amazon but instead he instilled confidence in me by telling me exactly what size I would have to reach to be a potential world record-holder. Brian is a very smart man, quiet and determined, and it took him only minutes to spot that I had already been toying with weights. 'No help at all', he told me and then offered to train me at Littleton Street Youth Centre, in an old leather factory in Walsall. When I turned up there for the first time I found I was the only girl among 20 or 30 men, some of whom were lifting enormous loads. Somehow, between my embarrassment and wonderment at being in such a place, I started exercising with my dinky little weights, working to a programme that Brian proposed for long-term development of a fast arm and strong legs and shoulders. He wanted power, bounce and speed. I've never been short of bounce or cheek although in that room of sweat, grunts and groans it was a while before I was confident enough to make much of a noise.

For all that I was improving, 1972 was a year of consolidation and also of acceptance by my parents that athletics was going to be important to me. They were pleased enough that I was going to a secretarial college and proud to read my name in Wolverhampton's evening paper, the *Express & Star*. Mum gave her shy grin when she saw that and I think the paragraph which recorded that I had won seven events at some small meeting did more than anything else to convince her that athletics was not a passing fancy to me. I also received my first English Schools gold medal, throwing my best yet, 43.06 metres, in Washington, Co. Durham, where among the company were David Ottley, Steve Ovett (first in the intermediate 800 metres) and Seb Coe (13th in the 3,000 metres). I have to admit I don't remember either Steve, who was already being hailed as a future star, or Seb, who certainly wasn't.

In 1973 I stopped playing at being an athlete and became the genuine article. The year started marvellously and got better and better until I knew I would be leaving for New Zealand and the Commonwealth Games in Christchurch. First, though, there was January and the Cosford Games, where I high-jumped 1.69 metres, still a personal record clearance, behind Barbara Inkpen's 1.80 metres, and ran a 58.3-second heat in the 400 metres. Cliff Temple reported in *Athletics Weekly*: 'Theresa Sanderson (16) flopped over a totally unexpected 1.69 to the delight of the local Wolverhampton and Bilston supporters; earlier in the day she had been a 400 metres finalist, after a 58.3 heat the night before. And if you think you know the name – yes, you do. She won the English Schools intermediate javelin title last year with a personal best of 43.06! If the pentathlon does develop, as has been speculated, into a contest involving 800 metres and javelin as well as standard events, here is a talent particularly worthy of every assistance and encouragement. Or, indeed, even if it doesn't'.

Soon afterwards, Tom McNab, reporting on an indoor pentathlon at Cosford on 27 January – I was fourth with 3,530 points – wrote: 'The best athlete pound for pound was undoubtedly Tessa Sanderson, a power-packed little athlete who could well high-jump 1.75 metres this year'. I enjoyed that, but 16 years later I have still to fulfil Tom's prophecy.

Brian claims that weight-training had no impact on my performances that season – perhaps it was just the fact that I was becoming naturally stronger and technically more proficient that led to a succession of improvements. I don't think so, though. He is a wood machinist by trade, an ingenious man who was often busy inventing training aids for me. The best items he came up with were wooden balls weighted with lead at one, two and three pounds, each designed to fit my throwing grip. He first brought them along when I was competing in the Midland senior championships at Warley and I was tickled pink to have the opportunity to throw them almost when and where I wished. Javelins have a nasty habit of being dangerous in the wrong hands and just plain awkward when you take them for a walk or on the bus. I was once stabbed between the toes when a girl dropped a javelin at Aldersley, while travelling on buses used to be very embarrassing: I would go upstairs and leave the thing downstairs.

During the year I was to increase my best distance progressively by more than 8 metres, good progress bearing in mind that the previous three years had brought me only an extra 12 metres. The outdoor season began in May and I achieved second place in the Midland pentathlon championship with 3,453 points which I then improved by 186 points to come fifth behind Mary Peters, nearly a thousand points ahead in the WAAA championships, once again at Warley. The English Schools senior javelin title fell to me with a then best throw of 48.26 metres which was perfect preparation for my first WAAA competition at Crystal Palace a fortnight later. As so often happens with young competitors, I expended my best efforts on qualifying and failed to follow 48.36 metres with anything better than 45.84 and seventh place. Sharon Corbett won both the Midland and the WAAA championships but I was not over-concerned once I had been selected for the European junior championships in Duisburg. The thought of travelling held a magic with which neither boys, discos nor money could compare. I admit, too, that to fly in a 'plane was far more rapturous a prospect than to throw a javelin. Perhaps it was not surprising that I did not do too well, although in fairness I was throwing an unfamiliar model of javelin. I reached the final but came 12th with a miserable 39.18 metres, well behind Khristova of Bulgaria, whose 54.84 metres put her out of my reach and even beyond the British senior record which I wasn't to break for two years. Duisburg, however, had an enormous effect on my life, for I had taken athletics seriously for the first time as I made my bid for the selectors' approval. I realised, too, that much as I liked being an all-round athlete the choice had to be made between javelin and pentathlon, a good decision that, as happens so often when you are young, was made mostly for the wrong reasons. I knew that there would be more trips as a javelin-thrower. With this in mind, in my spare time I either trained or watched television, except when I went to the pictures with Pat so that she could sneak out and see her boyfriend. Sonia Lannaman, who had recently moved from Solihull club to be coached by Charles Taylor, was quickly becoming my closest pal, a relationship that grew until we were practically regarded as sisters by our club-mates at Wolverhampton and soon even by team officials at international fixtures. She is a superb sprinter and you will find her next to me on almost every picture taken at the time. Sonia trained systematically and, now that John Moogan had quietly convinced me that this was the only route to success, I was in a receptive frame of mind when I witnessed similar routine work by such young runners as Steve Ovett, who was as precocious about his near-shoulder length hair as he was his talent.

Back from Duisburg, I added another 10 centimetres to my javelin best and ten days later added another 93 points to my highest pentathlon total. To say I was confident as I headed down for the Commonwealth Games trials at Crystal Palace on 6 October would not be strictly accurate – I felt ready to take on anyone and put up a good show, but that was all. New Zealand wouldn't be seeing this happy young miss. Sure enough, Sharon Corbett and Pru French came out with 50 metres plus in the first round and by the fourth round I was throwing for respectability when, I don't quite know why, all the Sanderson cogs worked in rhythm and I tossed that javelin 51.34 metres for the upset victory of the meeting. Wow! I rang home and told Mum: 'It's me ... I won. Can you believe it?'. Then came a six-day wait to see if the selectors had the nerve to pick an 18-year-old unknown from Wood End, Wednesfield. They did, bless their hearts.

Of all the games I have been to, the Commonwealth Games in Christchurch in January, 1974, were the loveliest. From the moment we were greeted at the airport by Maoris throwing flowers to the last strains of 'Now Is The Hour' at the closing ceremony, I was one star-struck girl suspended in my own heaven. Yes, there were a few tears – I am not often short of those – at a half-inch misjudgement that cost me a medal, but New Zealand breathed its sweetest perfumes of kindness and friendliness upon us and I was enchanted.

There were no great expectations of me but I thought there was a chance of a medal because, with the exception of Petra Rivers and Jenny Symon, two Australians, and our girls, the Commonwealth is not famous for breeding javelin-throwers, or competitors of quality or quantity in any field event. The subjects of what was once the British Empire are almost as suspicious of ladies with muscles as they are of non-English speakers. I don't mind being an underdog, especially if I am an underdog with the potential to beat the top dog and so, in my heart of hearts, I nurtured hopes of returning to Mum, Dad, the family and my club with a medal of some description. It should have been so, too. My first efforts were not at all impressive, although a valid 46.80 metres at least put me on the electronic scoreboard. Then, just as in the trials, I felt everything flow, a few moments when each new movement is an extension of the last, and with a fierce roll of my right arm the javelin hissed into the sky. 'That's it', I was thinking as a tiny doubt began to grow. I looked down and saw that my toe had just broken the line. Sure enough, a red flag appeared and with it went my chance of a medal. Later I managed 48.54 metres to come a very bedraggled fifth.

Nothing in my life had hurt quite like this. Because I was so young, I hadn't the experience to pull myself together and say: 'Come on girl, keep calm, have another go'. I could think only of the piece of bad luck that, in the end, cost me a silver medal. Naturally, my heartbreak was displayed to all who tried to comfort me as big tears but one person was not impressed at all. Nelson Neale, a kind lady generally, decided on this occasion that she had to be cruel. Even now I am not sure she was sensible in telling me: 'Don't be such a baby. You are young and you can have a go next time'. I thought then 'How can she say those things?' but I vowed that in four years' time I would return to Wednesfield as Commonwealth champion, so I suppose Nelson knew what she was doing. She died a few years ago, and was mourned as a magnificent worker and a helpful if sometimes scatterbrained lady even by those who were not fully sympathetic to her traditional standards, which I was. Her club, Birchfield Harriers, named a new stand after her.

Freda Clarke was team manager in Christchurch with Nelson as her number two. Their priority was to protect the girls, not always easy but essential for their good and the peace of mind of parents at home. There were lots of high spirits around, quite a few wolves and the possibility of late nights, drink and going off the rails. Not many do – certainly I wasn't one of them for at that time I don't think I had ever had a boyfriend although I was very fond of a lad called Anthony Clacken to whom I later became engaged. I did have lots of pals in athletics, such as Glen Cohen, Bill and Peter Tancred and Barry Williams to chat to, laugh with and ask advice of. I shared a room with Sue Mapstone and Sue Pettit, 400-metre runners, but my particular friends were Sonia and Donna Hartley. I was also proposed to by no less a man than Filbert Bayi. I suppose I was starstruck at the time and Filbert was so handsome I could hardly take my eyes off him. Whether or not he really meant to marry me and take me to live in Africa with him I am not sure, but the conditions in which he proposed may have led him to believe I was something that I most definitely am not: a practically-minded farmgirl. Peter Tancred and Barry Williams had somehow managed to become involved in a sheep-shearing contest in the athletes' village and when they spotted me in a halter-top shirt there were threats of the sort I will leave you to guess at which compelled me to join in. There was no alternative but to grab hold of a stupid, stubborn sheep and try to strip its wool. I was in the middle of making a mess of this, filthy, sticky and hot, when Filbert popped his question. I nearly popped my mind ... and then made my excuses. At that age I was literally an innocent abroad, a jumble of fibre and feelings that had still to be shaped. Yet there were intrusions into my fantastic land, and one of them, the death of Lillian Board, moved me greatly. She came – dressed, I remember, in a pink outfit – to Aldersley when I first started there and I was a little awestruck. The nation followed the escalating tragedy of her illness with a slightly macabre fascination, until the news of her death was broken to me, among millions of others, by Gordon Honeycombe on ITN.

My special admiration was reserved for Verona Elder and Sonia in the British team; for John Carlos, Lee Evans and Tommy Smith among the world-famous. I was not concerned with the Black Power salutes for, to be honest, I didn't understand what they were saluting about. Later I did, of course, but I have never been a political person – it was their great talent and good looks that I really liked!

In Christchurch, the Queen hosted a garden party with Prince Charles. Among the masses who cheered and jostled around her, I was cheeky enough to step up to Prince Charles and pin an England team badge on his lapel. Last year I reminded him of it and he actually remembered the occasion so I asked him whether he had kept the badge in his jewel box. He chuckled at that. What poise the Royal Family had and what an innocence there was in this, one of the last places on earth where good manners and respect for other people went hand-in-hand with high spirits and relaxed behaviour. Is it like that still? I hope so. I left a little piece of my heart there. It isn't exactly easy to win a Commonwealth gold medal, as I was to find out in Edmonton, and yet the Games are always fun, whether we win or lose. To begin with, all the participants mingle freely, talk the same language, with the exception of the odd Indian, African or, some might say, Australian, and exchange badges and badinage. Then there are no barriers of colour, creed or country so that people just view each other as human beings who happen to be great, good or average athletes. Indeed, some of the runners are just plain bad but nevertheless come along to soak up the atmosphere. The survival of the Games is extremely important to the future of the Commonwealth in which the bonds are loosening year by year. It would be a dreadful pity if they were allowed to die or if boycotts wrecked them: they provide an identity beyond continents for people brought up with sound principles.

The next two years were a period of consolidation for me. All through this time John and Brian worked hard to keep me occupied in spite of distractions and my reluctance to build myself into a sturdier specimen of womanhood. I saw no real reason to change my shape whereas Brian knew that I might look good but that would never get me far enough in the javelin. A bit of a gentle persuader is Brian, who chipped away at my doubts, convincing me that I wasn't a commodity or a car body. 'You are,' he said, 'a young lady and a very attractive one. If you want to be the super javelin-thrower you keep saying you do then some muscular development has to take place in certain areas, such as the shoulders. I promise that you will not lose your femininity.' What a smooth talker! He would not lie to me, never has, and eventually he convinced me that my five feet six inch frame needed to weigh up to 11 stones, two stones more than I weighed at the time. He clinched the argument by pointing out that whenever I wished to return to my pre-javelin self I could run off the muscle built up in six months in six weeks, provided I was careful about my diet. He devised particular exercises and invented a pulley system in the gym, high in the rafters so that I could reach up and copy exactly the action required on delivery. Brian understands my psychology and is clever at tempting me to lift weights that normally I would reject with a shrug. He flatters me by saying that I have world-ranking potential at the snatch and brings out my competitive instinct by suggesting lifting matches. He's a bag of tricks, too, substituting 20-kilogram weights for tens when he thinks I am not watching. I've caught him doing that, crafty devil. We do not fall out because I know he has my welfare at heart and I trust him. When I was 19 he must have been anxious to see results and yet he would never load me down, telling me he was a long-term man. His idea was that my natural strength would come through with careful management. I am certain he is right and for that reason I was not a one-night whizz-bang.

The target for 1974 was Sue Platt's British record which stood at 55.60 metres. In the 12 years since it seems to have shrunk progressively faster, but then, although it was apparently well in range, it was frustratingly unreachable for some while. I did, however, open the season with a personal record that, because of circumstances, I don't think I shall ever beat. At the WAAA pentathlon championships I recorded 3,877 points, comprising a 14.9-second 100 metres hurdles, 10.21-metre shot-putt, 1.68-metre high-jump, 5.55-metre long-jump and 25.6-second 200 metres, and finished seventh. Five days later I threw a UK junior record of 52.36 metres as a prelude to my first senior international match, a four-corner event involving Britain, West Germany, Italy and Romania in Bucharest where I finished fifth. This was the life for me, swanning around Europe, 18 years old and agog at cities that I thought I would never forget. The reverie was to end when I encountered the prodigious Ruth Fuchs for the first time, one sight of her technique confirming what in my heart I must have known: that she was not so much in a different league to me as three arcs further on. It was in a match with East Germany at Crystal Palace on 19 June that I recorded my puny 51.22 metres against her 65.58 metres – now that was a real target, a target that flesh and blood created and, therefore, one that could and would be beaten. I crept away, knowing that if I continued to be selected there would be nowhere to hide from this woman whom I still regard as the finest javelin-thrower of them all. She was big, fast and strong; whether she took anabolic steroids I do not know, but as the use of such drugs is normal in East Germany, it would not be too surprising if she did.

In Stockholm I threw 10 centimetres over the 54-metre qualifying distance for the European Games a month later and so I went to Rome, one of the babies of a team that included no fewer than six of my Wolverhampton team-mates: Glen Cohen, sprinter Don Halliday, Bill Tancred (discus), Mike Bull (pole vault), and my two special friends Verona Bernard and Sonia. Of the hopeful half-dozen only Glen returned with a gold medal, for an exhilarating win in the 4×400 relay, and of the whole British team I am the only person who still regularly competes as an international. It makes me sound like an old lady. I failed to reach the final by just one place, coming 13th with 53.28 metres. This was a shade disappointing rather than disastrous and I learned a good deal from Ruth Fuchs, whose winning effort of 67.22 metres broke the world record. Back home, I closed the season with my third UK junior best, 55.04 metres.

It would be best to pass lightly over 1975. My most memorable achievement was winning a *Sunday Times* award as the ideal all-round sports girl, given to me, the newspaper said, for being multi-talented and totally feminine. They did a big spread of pictures of me and provided a great boost to my career. That was very generous of them. Meanwhile as a multi-talented, totally feminine 19-year-old I worked hard as a copy typist at Eaton Ltd, of Wednesfield, and trained in most of the other waking hours. It didn't bother me. A crowd of us were eating fish and chips as we made our way home at about nine o'clock one night when there, in a doorway, I spotted Nogin. Actually, it took me a while to recognise her, for my old throwing rival had become a policewoman.

I was coming to realise that John Moogan's demand for absolute dedication was not the selfishness of a coach who wanted to spoil his athlete's fun. Dedication is the athlete's burden: work, train, home to bed and up to work again. It is hard in every event but for throwers a little bit more so because of all the weight training and technique that must be acquired. I will go a lot further and say that because javelin-throwing calls also for co-ordination at speed it is the most exacting of all.

There are three phases after achieving momentum: the right heel has to come in, then turn out, bringing the hip into line, finally pushing the shoulder and arm through for the ejection. It sounds relatively easy but it isn't. Speed is essential, not bulk, an attribute that suits me. The Greek Anna Verouli had been a very sharp, co-ordinated girl and then appeared in Los Angeles as a great knot of weight and muscle so that she almost waddled down the run-up. Without the smooth speed, fast cruise rather than a sprint, the throw becomes akin to putting the shot because it is body leverage that is required not bulk thrust. Fast bowling at cricket is similar and so is smashing at badminton because the player must get over the top of the shuttlecock. To me, there is a rare beauty in javelin-throwing: it is hard work but I have found it impossible to give up.

I had, however, very nearly finished with trying to be a pentathlete, warming up at Warley in May for an unsatisfying total of 3,521. Sue Platt's record seemed almost to be retreating from me, for although I won my first WAAA senior title with 54.40 metres I failed to improve on distance for the first year since I started. Yes, I did become British number one, although I never really cared about that, my eyes being on the world scene and particularly on Ruth Fuchs who proceeded to parade her pedigree skills three times before me; 61.48 to my 50.08 in an international in Dresden, 63.20 to 52.70 in the Europa Cup semi-final in Dresden and 64.80 to 48.72 in the Europa final in Nice. The gulf was widening as I was supposed to be getting stronger. It was, however, the hush before the explosion.

In my life there have been six key throws: the Commonwealth trials in 1973; the British record in 1976; the first time I beat Ruth Fuchs; the Commonwealth winner in Edmonton; Moscow 1980 and Los Angeles 1984. I built up to the record with a consistent set, three of them beyond my 1974 personal best, until the Olympic trials at Crystal Palace on 11 June. With 55.02 metres in Split, Yugoslavia, I had leapfrogged the Olympic qualifying standard and so I was thoroughly relaxed as I went into the competition. The javelin arced to 56.14 and, as I said at the time, I had broken a tremendous barrier for myself. 'The wind was just right, gusting against, and as it went out it felt so quick I could feel myself going with it' – that's what I said afterwards, still in a bit of a gust myself. Still, you can understand why I was so pleased. Then Sue Platt came along to meet me, commenting that the eight-year-old record had been too long on the books and needed beating. She reckoned I would look back and wonder why it had been so hard but the all-time British lists show why: she is still the seventh best thrower in our history.

And so to Montreal and the Olympics. They started badly because of a dreadful injury to Sonia and not even a new UK record could revive spirits dulled by overcrowded conditions, poor organisation, massive security and the capture of only one athletics medal, a bronze for Brendan Foster, from the entire team. With that as a yardstick, you can see just how well Britain did in Moscow and Los Angeles. I had just finished competing when I was informed that Sonia had been carried out of the stadium. The poor lass was in tears – I gave her a hug but she was inconsolable for a while and no wonder. It was soon obvious that the hamstring tear was not repairable for competition at those Games. Less obviously, something in Sonia's mental make-up has remained beyond repair, for so abundant was her talent for running fast that she should have been the world's best. She needed someone to drive her all the time – self-motivation was never a feature of her quiet personality which not far below the surface is rather defensive. Was the killer instinct missing? I am not sure, yet I do know that to reach and then stay at world class in any sport you have to be a bit greedy, even selfish. There are times when I have not been very happy with things I have had to do that were best for me and my future, although not necessarily for anyone else. Refusing to compete for your club is a particular problem but there are occasions when not to do so could affect your performance in an important event shortly afterwards – finding the dividing line between commitments and duty to your own talent can be very difficult, especially as your friends are anxious that you should be winning team points. Club officials do not often understand, either, although Bob Roberts did and, in a peculiar way, that put even more pressure on me.

In Montreal, although I may have looked like a little-girl-lost among the giants around me, I was in the process of toughening my attitudes. Waiting in the entrance tunnel before the qualifying round I was asked by one of the medal favourites, Karen Smith, if I was a sprinter. No one, it appeared, had seen a five feet six inch, nine-stone javelin-thrower before. I said: 'Am I, hell!' and, snap, I was in the proper, aggressive state of mind. The tunnel may be the final place in which to get yourself together, and although it was a nerve-wracking time for a girl of 20, the youngest there in fact, I knew I had done my training and a good warm-up so I thought 'Now I am going out there to fight'. Out in the stadium, I felt so tiny and slightly vulnerable, but I was also confident and the result was that, partly as a reaction to Karen's clumsy remark, I did well. My first throw was ruled to have landed flat and I summoned all my resolve to put in a second that flew 57.18 metres to set a new British record and earn me seventh place among the qualifiers. This was followed by 57.00 metres in the final for tenth behind Fuchs, who won with 65.94

metres. My efforts should have killed off forever the accusation that I flunked at major events: after all, with the exception of Christchurch and my peeping toe I had either won competitions or broken records each time I had gone to the runway in an important event. I was to find that killing off rumours is a damned sight harder than starting them.

The athletes' quarters in Montreal were diabolical – and that isn't too strong a word. A shade better than in Bucharest a year earlier, maybe. When I tell you that in Romania the East German team stole our beds one night and that there were ants in every one of them in the new quarters you have some idea of what scale of quality I am talking about. Our management people on that occasion threatened to take the team home if no better rooms could be found. It was in Bucharest, incidentally, that Sonia grew so cold waiting for the starting gun in the relay that she was putting on her tracksuit trousers when the starter fired the pistol. She pulled them up quickly and ran hell for leather.

In Montreal, there were ten of us to a room and we hadn't the faintest idea where we were to put our clothes. It was a case of picking up the nearest pair of knickers you could find and wearing them. Imagine, ten girls trying to look beautiful for the disco or banquet and there we were, struggling to find our drawers – Beverley Callender couldn't find hers so she sent me to pick up a pair that had fallen off a washing line. And our uniforms: well, they were so out of fashion we looked like a bunch of old ladies going for a Sunday walk. The dresses were ankle-length and we spent half our time pinning them up. As for the hats, they flopped over our faces and completed a picture that belonged to a 1920s church parade. You can imagine how it was when we tried to make a stylish and classy impression: just embarrassing. As for the athletics, I was struck by Don Quarrie and Ed Moses, who was just a whip of a guy, so fluent and so smooth. Lasse Viren was the name on everyone else's lips it seemed, but I do not remember much about him or the fuss that grew around alleged blood doping. I didn't really understand what that was although the talk of anabolic steroids and suchlike was beginning to catch my attention. If those same

Olympic Games were held tomorrow I think I would have been able to pass down the row of event finalists and pick out exactiy the people whom I felt were using them. At the time, the thought of drugs frightened me.

Montreal had spoiled the Olympic fairytale for this lively young lady from Wednesfield. Security, officiousness, red tape and low-grade living conditions were not something I expected from the greatest show on earth. Even so, I grew up a couple of years in those three weeks and at home I was to win the WAAA championship comfortably and complete my main programme with a new UK record, 57.20 metres, at the British International Games at Crystal Palace. I have to admit that by this time I was looking for better competition than could be provided within our shores, a requirement that exceeded the bounds of official imagination. England had been good enough for a hundred years, why not now? I was to show why the next year.

CHAPTER THREE

Good Vibrations

I was discovered in 1977: one of those overnight successes who tread the boards, or runways, for years before the general public becomes aware, on the evidence of one performance, that someone has something to offer. The breakthrough came on 17 July; to friends and close observers it was obvious five weeks earlier that Brian's weight training in tumbledown Littleton Street and John Moogan's expertise had combined to polish my talent to the level at which I was able to play a part on the world stage. Ultimately, I am sure any good coach would agree, it is, though, the athlete who must develop his or her own approach, remaining continually alert to the little points in competition that will make the difference. There are no better learning processes than those of experience and self-discovery as I found out by teaching myself to do the Fosbury Flop in the high-jump.

I began the outdoor season with my usual WAAA pentathlon and a month later Warley was the scene for what was the best double of my 21 years, a new UK record of 58.90 metres for the javelin and 61.9 seconds for the 400 metres hurdles. A week later at Cwmbran in Wales I improved on both, beating 60 metres for the first time, by 24 centimetres, and coming third in the one-lap hurdles in 60.46 seconds. The winter hurdling I had undertaken in the hangar at RAF Cosford had really paid off, even though I admit my stride pattern was all over the place. At the time it was my intention to take the event seriously but the truth is that eight years later the Cwmbran time which won me third place at the UK championships remains my fastest. And the second to last time I ever tried it. Then, during six days at the end of the month, there occurred two unrelated but significant meetings. At the Debenham Jubilee

Games, I met a dark, shy girl with whom I had an initial rapport, Fatima Whitbread. She was 16 then, already eager to learn and competitive with it. Her best throw reached 42.88 metres, mine 57.76, a victory for me that meant nothing to either of us. It was about this time, although it might have been a year later, that I wrote to her wishing her a wonderful career in the hope that two top-class javelin-throwers would spearhead a revolution in the event. It has. If only the circumstances had been better.

In Dusseldorf on 1 July, I proceeded to break the Commonwealth record with a pitch of 64.42 metres, more than four metres beyond my best. Perhaps even more important was that among those watching was Michael Samuelson, whose company was filming out there. At the turn of the year, I had changed jobs, moving into a flat in Telford New Town, Shropshire, where I became an audio typist and assistant to the Head of Sport of the Development Corporation, mainly because the job allowed me more time to train. Michael thought it a pity that I remained short of the kind of money which would take the anxiety out of my daily existence and with wonderful generosity persuaded five other members of the Variety Club of Great Britain to repeat his offer of £1,000 each for a three-year sponsorship. All they ever asked was that I should write them the occasional postcard telling them what I was doing and where. Needless to say, those notes were sent with love and kisses, thereby setting the scene for a shocking scenario about which I write later in this book.

John, meanwhile, had managed to obtain video film of Ruth Fuchs in action a year earlier and, noting her balanced speed on the run-up, we had introduced one or two changes to my own approach. In 16 years of javelin training, she is the only competitor to have had that kind of influence on me and so, when I flew to Dublin for the European Cup semi-final on 17 July, I was still in some awe of her. I took my own javelins to Ireland and you can imagine how annoyed I was when the meeting director ruled that we all had to use the ones supplied which happened to be of the same make to those the East Germans used. By the second round all my aggression was channelled into throwing the thing as far as I could, so I took an enormously long run-up, went hell for leather, and sent my much-abused javelin flying to 67.20 metres. I don't think I have ever had so much aggression before or since and it was more than enough to beat Fuchs, whose best was 64.46 metres. I raised my arms in the air. 'Sod you lot', I thought. 'I've beaten the Olympic champion.' When Seb Coe won the Los Angeles Olympic 1500 metres he gestured angrily at the Press because he had been written off by them. The same sort of emotion filled me with controlled fury that night. If it could be manufactured, it would be worth millions.

Ruth came over to congratulate the winner, me, not something she was in the habit of doing as she had not been beaten for about four years. I found her gracious then and have done ever since because she reappears from time to time as a team delegate. The East Germans could not believe a nine-stone slip of a lass had beaten their superstar. When they heard my training amounted to one weight training and two throwing sessions a week, I was immediately invited to go over there and train with them. No fear! I think they were more interested in finding out what made me tick than in encouraging me to improve, especially as technically I was nothing like as accomplished as I am now. Anyway, I like England and I particularly like my colleagues on the British team. Athletics demands an increasing amount of time and effort, sheer dedication really, from its international representatives. To be winners we have to look after our own interests first and while I would not suggest that is reason for ignoring the needs of other people, when it comes to athletics-related matters there is one golden rule: will it help you? You do not need to be clever to understand why – the best way to support the team and the best way to give enjoyment to audiences is to win. And you will not do that often enough if you are at everyone's beck and call. I know that to my cost because I competed far too often last year when I was not in the physical condition I should have been in and had not attuned my mind to a tough programme.

Nevertheless, I am a team girl at heart. We lost that night in Ireland and we were all dejected, especially as our men had done well and qualified for the final. There is always a sense of togetherness once we know what it is to wear the red, white and blue vests. I have never for one moment regretted competing for a British team although overtures were made to me to follow Marilyn Neufville, who left England to run 400 metres for Jamaica. That was in 1974 before the Commonwealth Games and I didn't know until much later that Sir Arthur Gold, then secretary of the AAA, had flown out early to talk to the Jamaican team management about Glen Cohen, who was in the same predicament, and me. We both held Jamaican as well as British passports and could have competed for either country. Sir Arthur must have put a stop to any possible negotiations because I had only one clue that such a move had been requested. A photographer at Cosford told me he hoped I wasn't going to do what Marilyn had. I thought 'how stupid' – it had never occurred to me and even if it had I would have remained here with my friends and family. I met Marilyn at a party Don Quarrie held in Christchurch and she said she had been harassed in England. I don't know how true that was but I suspect that she was not altogether happy that she had made the right decision. She had such exceptional talent it is to be regretted that she just faded from the scene. She would have made the crucial difference in Dublin.

I have been fortunate enough to win several big competitions. That has made me proud – not so much for Britain, that is only a minor part of it – but primarily because it is a goal achieved despite all the problems, and also because those people I feel close to will be a mite happier for a while. Team-mates are usually nearest to you at the time of victory and I really value their reaction and, when warranted, esteem. Although I have had a major dispute with Marea Hartman, the WAAA secretary, that might have ended in the courts if she had not apologised, I do feel she has performed a remarkable service to women's athletics in this country, especially in helping, in her Mother Hen way, the younger girls. She will be missed when she leaves because she knows her sport is not fundamentally about commercialism and subventions, power-broking, jazzy promotions or, worst of all, meaningless races. It is purely and simply about the testing of one athlete against other athletes, with the stopwatch and measuring tape as interested parties.

Young people coming into athletics now are going to miss the *esprit de corps* of being true sportsmen winning for the pleasure of it. Don't misunderstand me, I am totally for the payment of athletes when rewards are supervised and shared in a fair manner and I do think the elite should receive higher fees just as they would in any other form of show business. Other sports are hard in their way but none demands the fitness and dedication of athletics. Golf may take up a lot of time although from some of the pot bellies I see around the courses most of the training is with the right elbow – golfers even have people to carry their bags around. Footballers seem to work a couple of hours each morning and lounge around for the rest of the day; cricketers to spend much of their time in the pavilion; and the other day I saw tennis players practising by having a gun shoot balls at their racquets. I wish I had some robot who would bring back my javelins, or perhaps I should teach a big dog to do it. For athletes who want to make it to the top, the whole training business is becoming tougher and tougher: nothing will stop the trend towards athletes becoming full-time, living on the dole in winter and their fees in the season. That is sad. It would not be asking too much of the athletics authorities to try to set up a register of employers who would allow athletes the necessary time off in return for publicity. I say this because I had a job right up to the Los Angeles Olympic Games and I would not have missed the comradeship for anything. I needed the money, too.

When athletes begin to earn their living solely from their sport, I suspect that athletics will become too serious for its own good: competitors auctioning their services to the highest bidder are not likely to make good company if they are in a poor streak. Nor might they be keen to compete for club or country at any meeting except major games when elsewhere they could be receiving hundreds, maybe thousands, of pounds. Then there could be questions, too, about their fitness. In Eastern Europe, there will be no such dissent from the party line and I think you could predict a decline in match results against the Communist Bloc within a few years. Mary Peters, the best team manager I ever had, retired because she was worried about what would happen when athletics became rich. Last season there was more than enough evidence to support the reasons for her unease. I have watched in horror some of the financial manipulation that has mocked the principles of fairness.

Back at Aldersley after my Dublin success, I was greeted by John Moogan who took me quietly aside and, after congratulating me for throwing really well, asked me a question that with a single blow shattered the relationship that had grown between me and him, and his family, over four years. 'You didn't take anything, did you?' he asked. My heart sank. I said: 'Don't be silly. I have never taken anything in my life and I never will'. He was relieved, I could see that, but he should have known me better and the question set off a chain of recriminations that made me wonder about many decisions that previously I had not concerned myself with. At first we both thought it was a temporary phase but the next year our connection was to be severed permanently.

I went to Helsinki for the World Cup final with a series of 60-plus throws behind me and the confidence gained from beating Fuchs for the only time in my life. Ruth avenged herself with a magnificent 68.92 metres to my 62.36 in Finland but Dublin had ensured my position as European representative in the World Cup three weeks later by which point I was beginning to tire. In between times I won the WAAA championships on the third of seven consecutive occasions and by such a distance that it was almost a formality. A year or two later I felt it incumbent upon me to write to Marea Hartman stating that it would be better if she imported a foreign thrower or two to liven up competition. She never did and, furthermore, in Olympic year she barred me from the event because my entry form arrived two days late. Three girls, Sonia Lannaman, Donna Hartley and I, and two men, Steve Ovett and Nick Rose, were selected for the team in Dusseldorf, a city I shall always remember for I associate it with Edwin Moses whom I met there and liked instantly. It was through his coach, a huge, pear-shaped man named Jackson, that I met Edwin, who in contrast is tall and slim. Jackson was characteristically lounging about the hotel one day – was there ever a man who looked less like a coach, let alone coach to the best 400 metres hurdler there is ever likely to be? – waiting to share the latest gossip. I asked him where Edwin was and he replied that he was in his room preparing to go and pray. This was not exactly the way athletes usually ready themselves for a race, and unfortunately I couldn't wait so it was after my event – I was third behind Fuchs and Nadyezhda Yakubovich – that finally we sat down on the edge of the arena and chatted. Edwin is one of the most warm, sincere people I have met and it angered me greatly when I read that stuff about him allegedly picking up a prostitute. He was cleared, of course, and I believe that someone had set out to tarnish a superstar. We had an affair but distances were too great and schedules never quite fitted in, so nothing came of it except my everlasting admiration for a man who has immense dignity and faith in the right things. He always kept in touch by letter, however, and I was deeply moved at the Olympic Games closing ceremony in Los Angeles when he stole up to me, put his arm around my shoulder and said that the greatest thing to happen to him in the Coliseum was watching me win my gold medal.

I had another less emotional entanglement in Dusseldorf – with the biggest T-shirt I ever saw. Helena Fibingerova, an immense, lovely lady, offered me hers. When I put it on, it was more like an overcoat. Fibingerova was the woman who, having won the world shot-putt title in Helsinki, decided that the way to celebrate would be to hug all the men around her. They scattered like autumn leaves but not before she had grabbed four or five of them and given them huge, Czechoslovakian kisses. I made her the star of the Games.

I have had several offers to go to America for a university scholarship. The upheaval was more than I could face and although I was tempted by the idea of warmer weather, and testing myself against such girls as Kate Schmidt, who threw a world-record 69.34 metres to my miserable 55.74 at Furth, West Germany, it was nothing more than a passing fancy. I suppose I was a little set in my ways and I also knew how important it was that British women's athletics should make a breakthrough in field events. This view was ratified by my election by the British Athletics Writers as Woman Athlete of the Year – the first time a thrower had been so honoured – shortly to be followed by the joint award of the Sybil Abrahams trophy to Sonia and me for outstanding performances during 1977. We went to Buckingham Palace for that one.

In spite of the heights I reached in 1978 when I won the Commonwealth gold medal and the European silver, there was a tarnishing of two relationships that caused me disappointment and hurt. It had become clear to both John and I that there would have to be a break-up and it was practically an unspoken agreement that after the Games in Edmonton, Canada, we would separate. He found coaching an international athlete as well as teaching and looking after his family had brought strains that could be relaxed only by sacrificing something: my coaching was that something. Brian, who respected John's abilities as much as I did, believes the fault was six of one and half-a-dozen of the other and I would not necessarily argue with that, except to say, as I have said before, that an athlete has to be greedy for undivided attention. The better he or she becomes the more this is so, particularly in events of technical intricacy. By the European championships in Prague I was at a loose end and as I knew Wilf Paish, the national event coach, quite well by then I asked him whether, if I was to lose my coach, he would be interested in replacing him. Wilf said he would love to help me. A fortnight later, I met John in the car park after an Aldersley training session and he commented that he was pleased but shocked I had done so well. Soon afterwards he wrote to say it would be better if I found another coach and from then on the split was official. I was very sad at the time. I contacted Wilf for what was to be the forging of our Olympic relationship, though not before many heartaches. Wilf has shared all of those, for it is a coach's misfortune – although some of them love the fatherly part – to have to listen and advise their athletes on almost every problem in their lives. At least they do if they are good, and Wilf is very good. Such a relationship is precious, based on 100 per cent honesty, but calling for tact, flattery, the occasional sharp word and constant support. The athlete shouldn't hide anything: there is a father-daughter bond between Wilf and I whereas with John it was more teacher-favourite pupil. Nevertheless, I retain enormous respect for his abilities.

My second disruption was with Sharon Colyear, a close friend whose beauty turned more than a few men's heads. Sharon had been chosen for the 4×100 metres team despite the fact that Wendy Hoyte had run slightly faster times, a close decision that others in the relay squad did not favour. I wasn't aware of this until on my way to compete I asked Sonia why the sprinters were being so moody. I suggested she, as the best sprinter, should go and talk to one of the team managers but before she could do so Marea Hartman, who is quite sensitive to this sort of problem, asked me why there were long faces around. I told her that she ought to see the relay girls because they were not happy with the composition of the quartet. So far as I was concerned, that was it. But Marea proceeded to call in each girl to ask them what was the matter, and the outcome was that Sonia and I were branded as the people who preferred Wendy. Sharon and I were close friends and I could not believe that she would accept that version. When she did, our friendship was ruptured. The other girls made it up but I thought 'If that is her opinion of me then I don't want to know'. Soon afterwards she married Bob Danville, captain of Wolverhampton and Bilston, and another friend with whom I had spent many happy times. I wasn't invited to the wedding at first and even Daley Thompson, who stayed at my place for the weekend as we were to do a television programme together, could not persuade me to accept an invitation that arrived far later than everyone else's. Damn my pride but I just could not accept. I sent a bouquet and wished the couple my love. It was the only friendship in athletics that I ever lost and even then we eventually got together again after Bob confided to Glen Cohen that they had discovered the truth. We are close friends again now, although we see little of each other because the Danvilles live in the States.

I showed no improvement that year on the Dublin throw, yet in 13 javelin competitions I won 11 and was second in two, both times to Ruth Fuchs. At Crystal Palace in the match with East Germany on 11 June, the results read Fuchs 66.26, Sanderson 60.68, Petra Felke 57.72 and Fatima Whitbread 51.80. The old and the new orders were meeting for Felke was in 1985 to become the first woman to throw beyond 75 metres while Fatima, as most people know, was to come second in the Helsinki world championships and third in Los Angeles. A few days before the match, Fatima had also beaten my aged-17 best with 53.88 metres – prodigious going – which plainly earmarked her as a great prospect.

Winning and losing. Rudyard Kipling advised us to treat those two impostors the same. That might have been all right for him, living comfortably under the Raj in India, but for we athletes the reality is to treat losing as an impostor and winning as a close friend. There had been no serious setbacks in my career until 1980. I had become a sporting celebrity, I suppose, but being well-known has never made the slightest difference to me because it is the inner person that matters. I come from a close-knit, happy-go-lucky family and I like to think they bred proper standards in me. I know I always hated housework and chores but I was made to do them by my Aunt Kitty who prided herself on being a tyrant, a fair tyrant maybe, but a lady who demanded and received deference. Only later was I to realise how important it was to know right from wrong, and to try to help other people, especially children. I honestly believe that I have attended more charity events and visited more homes and schools than anyone in athletics, with the possible exception of Steve Ovett.

Anyway, armed with integrity and a combative spirit it is possible to overcome any adversity. But first came my morsels of fame. Edmonton, Alberta, was the scene of one of them. The Commonwealth Games of 1978 confirmed my view that as a meeting of athletes they are unbeatable, providing a perfect compound of great company and good competition. We stayed in the university campus of this oil-rich city which has largely succumbed to the American way of life while remaining practically the last outpost of Canadian civilisation before the wilds of the Yukon. I went there as favourite for the gold medal, my longest throw being nearly 10 metres further than that of my closest rival. Among the younger competitors there to gain experience was Fatima Whitbread, with whom I shared some lovely times, including wild 'look, no hands' bicycle rides. She was cheerful company and enjoyed herself so much that I am surprised she later cut herself off from the team, along with her mother, Margaret, who became national javelin coach.

I also came to know Wilf Paish better. He was national field events coach until after the Moscow Olympics and in Edmonton the inexhaustible little man seemed intent on covering every inch of the campus in pursuit of someone or something. My event was on 10 August and the result was the one most people expected. What a relief! Once again I had killed the bogey that I was the girl who 'toed the line' at Christchurch – or so I thought. On a glorious last day for Britain, Sonia won the 100 metres and we returned home to Wolverhampton as the golden twins. For years our careers had run parallel courses, starting years earlier in a junior championship when I had three no-throws and she made three false starts. A sad little pair of failures we were that day. But in Edmonton – well, what a contrast!

In the field events especially there is a marked difference in standards between the Commonwealth and Europe as a result of which for a long time East Germany and Russia have been dominant. I knew that I would do exceptionally well to finish in a medal-winning position in the European championships, which took place in the Czechoslovak capital where the welcome was polite and the security in our prison-like athletes' village overdone. I have always hated throwing in rain or the cold and Prague this early autumn was very wet and decidedly chilly. My final was on 1 September and the weather was more miserable than ever. Even through three layers of tracksuits I was soaking by the time we had taken our warm-up throws. I found it difficult to land positively on the foot that anchors the throw and, furthermore, the binding of all the javelins was as slippery as a bar of soap. I was not the only one unable to take a firm grip and performances, except for one from Ruth Fuchs, were ordinary. She won with a magnificent 69.16 metres while I was second on 62.40, pleased that I had relegated several highly-ranked women into minor positions.

Few people in the West realise how well our living standards compare with most of the rest of the world's. In Prague, you had to ask for butter to spread on your bread while the egg soup appeared to have been created by a chef with a sense of humour. None of us could swallow the soggy blobs that floated in warm water, while I swear the best meat came from horses. Our quarters were like a prison and I felt trapped in the thick blackness of the night. Perhaps these privations helped me concentrate on the battle to come.

I returned home rather expecting good reviews in the newspapers but found myself much better appreciated by the Crystal Palace crowds than by the reporters in Prague who dismissed in a few paragraphs what many experts felt had been a breakthrough performance. Only Ron Pickering made much of my achievement which was new to Britain. He described my silver medal as probably the most important precedent for many years. I felt, however, that a few other words of praise would have done a lot for javelin-throwing – I had, after all, become the first British woman to win a European throwing medal– and they also would have helped me in my search for financial assistance. Few people have any idea of just how hard-up athletes are. Although my friends in the Variety Club were very generous, I needed more assistance than I could possibly ask of them. I must say, too, that I was privately upset that I was passed over as Sportswoman of the Year, a title won by Sharron Davies, the swimmer, who did well in the Commonwealth Games but in world terms hardly rated. I hated sitting there waiting for the result, half expecting, half dreading, the outcome. It was even worse when I was announced as runner-up. I think I have matured since then, however, and I hope I would not take such a let-down quite as seriously if it were ever to occur again.

Before that point, however, I had won an eight-nation tournament in Tokyo in September, and had discovered that my apparently inexhaustible appetite for travelling could be more than satisfied by such a long journey, never mind the quantities of fish that appeared at every meal.

Up to 1983 when the world championships were introduced, every odd year was fallow. So it was with 1979, in which year a gaggle of competitions were enlivened by the European championships and little else. It was a year of looking forward to the Olympic Games in Moscow when I would test myself against Fuchs,

Todorova, Maria Colon and all of the up-and-coming throwers who had lately arrived on the scene. My great difficulty was in training. Wilf lived in Leeds and we could manage to meet only once or twice every month and so it fell to John Trower, an international thrower himself, Steve Pearson and Simon Osbourne to help me through vital sessions in the winter. Wilf recognised that technically I was no more than adequate and that arm pains were being caused by a bad carry of the javelin, a hangover from my days at Ward Bridge where I had learned to hold low and raise as I was about to throw. He tried to iron that out and to put some discipline into my last stride. It was tremendously long and, though it gave me leverage, I could not pull out of it. It had the effect of delivering the javelin far too high into the sky, rather like a kite that swirls upwards and falls suddenly with a bump.

Telford Development Corporation helped me by ordering a special tartan runway half a mile from my new flat which overlooked the spreading new town. I was thereby saved the 32-mile round trip to Wolverhampton and the even longer journey to Walsall, a detail which might not mean much to non-athletes but to field-eventers is such a time-saver that it can make the difference between a silver medal, won by David Ottley who joined the Development Corporation four years ago, and a place looking on enviously from the athletes' enclosure. Furthermore, I had very special aid – a mongrel terrier called Suzie who somehow ended up as my flat-mate. What a crazy dog! She was such a pal that she even learned to run for my javelin, pick it up and bring it back. Golfers will know what I mean when I say she saved me hours of tedious retrieval. She was, however, rather a loony as dogs go, disappearing for days on end and then turning up, on one occasion as far away as Cannock, about 15 miles from Telford. I loved that beat-up old mongrel and when she vanished for the final time it broke a piece off my heart.

It was at about this time that I fell deeply in love for the first time. I have no wish to open old wounds and only insofar as it had a bearing on my life will I say very much. Sonia and I did much of our winter training in the chill old hangar at RAF Cosford which has for years served as the only indoor athletics arena in Britain. I was trying sprint starts under the tuition of her coach, Charles Taylor, and had bent down to adjust my blocks. I looked through my legs and spotted a few RAF men staring at me. I thought 'Cheeky devils, what are you doing there?' then forgot them for a while as we did some work. Later we started chatting with a group who were pulling our legs about boyfriends when I realised that I had seen one of them, Maurice Ducass, with a Chinese girl. That started another joking session and a few days later he and I went searching in my car for a physiotherapist to treat a sore tendon I had collected somehow. We knew his address in Stafford but never found him so we went to a bar for a drink and from that moment on there was an understanding between us. We did not kiss or even touch at that time. It wasn't necessary.

The affair ended exactly a year later in the same setting, Cosford, where he was stationed. It had been idyllic for the most part, not least because his family, especially his mother Joyce and father Rennie, were warm and lovely people from Liverpool. On the way to meeting them for the first time, he told me they were fans of mine and had just watched me on *Superstars*. No doubt he meant to put me at my ease but as I had just turned the rowing event into nautical chaos, he was not very successful. Not usually the silent or even subdued type, I experienced shyness for one of the few times of my life before that meeting. Joyce and I were soon the closest of friends, however, and it was not long before Maurice said to her: 'If I don't marry Tessa, I'll marry a queen'.

I think he meant it. He was a gentle, loving man who made me feel like a million dollars. His mother gave me the St Christopher chain I still wear in all my competitions, and Maurice bought me earrings shaped into the Pisces symbol to celebrate my birth sign. Those old Hollywood war films used to show heroes dressed in uniform, handsome and ready to steal a girl's heart. That was how Maurice looked when he set off to work from my flat – and how he looked when he returned home, not from war, but from the office. He would stand to attention so that I could admire him, knowing that we shared a secret: beneath the airforce blue jacket was as rumpled a shirt as any in the service. I was hopeless at ironing shirts. Perhaps the iron was cold but he had my love to keep him warm.

I lost one of the earrings and maybe that was a sign that we were drifting apart. To this day, I don't know why it happened. Not the real reason. He did not have another girlfriend and I certainly wouldn't have two-timed him, so I can only surmise that he could not handle the way my life was. We decided to meet to try to sort things out and concluded that we should part. It was the saddest day of my life but it had to be. I still regard Maurice's family as my second family, people with whom I know I can always relax.

I began the 1979 season with a 62.40-metre throw in May and during the following weeks improved to 64.82 in Bucharest and 65.34, my best effort since Dublin, in Furth, West Germany. The athletics world was becalmed before the storm of the Moscow Olympic Games of 1980 and so, although my third in the major event of the year before, the European Cup final in Turin, was no triumph, Wilf and I were quietly contented with what I had achieved. Turin, as far as I was concerned, was notable only for the defeat of Fuchs by Eva Raduly, a Romanian, whose 66.28 in the fifth round beat the East German's first and best attempt by 82 centimetres. My bronze was won with 62.38 metres.

At least there was more competition at home. Fatima did well to break my old junior record with 56.66 metres, the same distance which she had attained in coming second to me in the WAAA championships. I was pleased that there was someone to share the burden abroad, to challenge me into better performances at home and just to be on the team to create a chance of popularising the javelin which, heaven knows, needed some help. For my part, I was finding that being coached by Wilf from Leeds was not ideal and it was just as well that John Trower, always ready to be at my side in Telford, and Brian Newman in Walsall, were so helpful.

Only days after the break-up of my affair with Maurice, a party of us flew to Australia to fulfil a short programme and to enjoy some sun as Britain headed for the depths of winter. It was a trip which lightened my own clouds, too, for on it as well were Daley Thompson, Allan Wells, Steve Ovett and long-jumper Sue Reeve, attended by manager Andy Norman, then a station sergeant with the Metropolitan Police at Purley, near Croydon, and currently the head of the British Athletics Promotions Unit. Andy, rapidly becoming the 'Mr Fixit' of the sport in Britain, carries as much weight physically as he does politically. He claims that he used to be a sprinter and I can only judge that they must have been slow races or he did not eat as much then as he does now. His appetite is colossal and Steve Ovett and I decided that Australia would be as good a place as any to slim him down a bit. For two days he dieted and then blew it with the most enormous breakfast I have ever seen. Andy is sharp and dynamic and, typical of a London policeman, loves smart wit, even directed at him. He was persuaded to go jogging with me and we ended up moving at such a crawl you would have thought he was in full uniform, boots and all. It was, however, one of the few occasions on which we were to be in step. I am grateful to him, and to the athletics board, for deciding that in 1980 they felt I was a good enough Olympic prospect to warrant a place among the elite squad. For once there were no money problems because the splendid six from the Variety Club were still sponsoring me. Wilf and I even had enough cash to go to America for winter training, something which was looked upon then as rather an extravagance. These days, Daley spends half his year in warmer climes.

As the season unfolded, it became apparent that I was throwing with special zest and that I would be second or third favourite behind Ruth Fuchs to win the Olympic gold medal that had now become my life's ambition. Every top-class athlete I know agrees that record-breaking is a runner-up to winning games medals, particularly if they are Olympic or world. Steve Cram says he would swap all of his world bests to be able to say that he was number one on the day destiny decided who would be Olympic champion. Records are always, eventually, expunged. That is predictable – even Bob Beaman's 'giant step for mankind' will be eclipsed, maybe even this century, and at sea level, not 7,000 feet up as his was. The record books show that we are all mortals whereas the history books declare that some deeds are at least grasping at immortality. So it is in sport. There are a select few who have broken significant barriers – Roger Bannister's four-minute mile immediately comes to mind – and remain legendary performers but it must be said that the short-cut to fame is by way of Olympic gold. Besides that, of course, the competition itself is magnificent. At times certain athletes fight shy of putting their reputation on the starting blocks, a few with good reason, although I will say that the grand prix series and consequent subvention prizes are invalidating even those. There is no giving the Olympic Games a miss though, not unless your country dictates it. Anyone who is anyone will be there and knowledge of this adds to the imperceptible increase in tension that begins two or three years before the Games themselves. True competitors love to line up with the best in the world, knowing that a victory in these circumstances is beyond personal value.

Yes, I would love to break the world javelin record and, indeed, I believe that I may do so yet. Certainly I have the throw in me as I have shown by occasionally producing a magical sky-searcher such as the one in Stuttgart on 5 June 1980. That was my Moscow throw exactly seven weeks too early. In a fixture with West Germany and Romania, I hurled 69.70 metres in my third round, a new Commonwealth record that would also have been a world best had not Fuchs extended the old one to 69.96 metres a few weeks earlier. I remember thinking as the javelin glinted into the distance that perhaps this was the first 70-metre throw in history – one of those historic barriers I mentioned a little earlier! – but it wasn't to be. I saw it fall just short of the white arc, a little sad and very pleased. As my fifth-round effort reached 68.54 metres and I beat Eva Raduly, the European Cup winner who herself attained a personal record of 67.22 metres, you can understand why my dreams of a place on the Moscow podium were difficult to suppress. They were promptly put into perspective, however, by a Russian woman of some mystery, Tatyana Biryulina, who from nowhere suddenly whacked out the 70-plus we had all been straining for. Biryulina, her best before 1980 a paltry 59.56, leapfrogged us all with 70.08 metres at Podolosk on 15 July. She came sixth in the Moscow games and then disappeared from competition.

Am I suspicious? I had experience myself, as have all javelin exponents, of catching the moment when the body and the javelin are one force in complete harmony, the throw almost an extension of myself. Wonderful. Perhaps that is what happened to Biryulina. Perhaps that is what happened to Russian high-jumper Rudolf Povarnitsin who, on 11 August 1985 in Donetsk, became the first man to break the 2.40-metre barrier when his previous best had been 14 centimetres lower. A case of history repeating itself, you might say.

I was not concerned with the decline in my form after Stuttgart. At Crystal Palace, I beat former world record-holder Kate Schmidt, throwing 64.68 metres, then took part in my final competition before Moscow when, also at Crystal Palace, I was second to Cuba's Maria Colon with 61.88 metres. I managed to alarm Fleet Street's correspondents by withdrawing with a 'dead arm' after a second-round 48.30 metres. This was hardly the image of a lady on the white charger astride which they would have wished me to enter the Lenin Stadium. Frankly, the arm troubled me, but then it had done so for years. I am not prepared to make excuses of that sort. I went to Moscow well-prepared, psychologically affected still perhaps by my broken love affair, but as far as my rivals were concerned, I knew I could knock 'em dead. Such dreams I had then.

CHAPTER FOUR

Moscow Failure

In Montreal, four years before Moscow, I witnessed one of the saddest moments I can remember from three Olympic Games. I had finished my event and went into the village restaurant where I sat next to a big African boxer. He turned his face away from me and, being the inquisitive sort, I asked him what the matter was. Then I saw that he was crying, slow tears rolling down his face. 'I've worked for four years to come here and fight,' he said, 'and today I was told I couldn't because my country is boycotting the Olympics. I'm going home without anything to show for it. Do these people care about athletes?' The answer has to be, unfortunately, that they don't give a damn. Boycotts are a nonsense, they do nothing and prove nothing, except that competitors can be used as pawns in political games. Now I am not a political person. I have views about helping poor people and conflicting views about the survival of the fittest and about the right to earn money. But Olympic or Commonwealth Games boycotts are just rubbish. Don't forget I am black and some of those boycotts have been in support of equal rights for black people, a movement for which I have the greatest sympathy.

What, though, did the Kenyans achieve by boycotting Montreal and then Moscow? Not an extra crust of bread, not a single new friend. Only the athletes and the public suffered, the athletes by missing the chance of competing and, in the case of the African runners and boxers, of winning at the greatest sports show in the world; the public because they lost the chance of watching or hearing of the feats of their own national heroes. How sad it is that a man like Henry Rono was never allowed to test himself against Lasse Viren, and how much it would have meant to Kenya, to impressionable young people and to national pride, if he had won a gold medal.

President Carter's boycott was even more stupid, and hypocritical, too. He demanded, and got, from athletes who were relatively helpless, something which he knew he could not get from businessmen; a gesture of contempt towards the Russians for their invasion of Afghanistan. Meanwhile, trade between the two countries was practically unaffected. Carter robbed Edwin Moses of his gold medal as surely as if he had been a Russian runner himself. I do not believe he or the stooges who carried out his wishes had the right to do that unless he was prepared to sever every trade and cultural link between the countries. As it was, a year later the United States sent an athletics team to Leningrad to compete in an international match. How preposterous! And, again, hypocritical! The Americans hoped they could sweet-talk the Soviet Union into bringing the Communist Bloc competitors to Los Angeles. They had no hope. Anyone who listened in Moscow knew that the chances of the Russians turning up were very slim indeed and as soon as I read about certain conditions being demanded by Moscow I had the feeling that we had been this way before. One boycott begat another, but one good thing resulted. The Russians, I believe, realise the futility of their gesture, just as the Americans did earlier. Afghanistan, after all, remains invaded; the streets of Los Angeles – for this was the Russian excuse – as crime-ridden as ever. And what about those countries who were carried along in the wake of the superpowers, or who refused to kow-tow to Washington or New York? For one reason or another, Britain for the most part and Romania refused at these Games to participate in boycotts. I understand that the Romanians have suffered a number of strange power-cuts as well as sanctions, both of Russian origin, but I bet the Bucharest man-in-the-street wouldn't forgo a moment of the Games or regret that his country exercised its right to make up its own mind. In Britain, we have two men, Seb Coe and Daley Thompson, who became double gold medal winners and there were also magnificent memories of Moscow for people such as Steve

Ovett and Allan Wells. Mine, as you will realise, were a good deal less satisfactory.

Mrs Thatcher attempted to impose her will on the sports organisations in Britain, and failed in all but three cases. She made forbidding noises but in the end had the good sense to stop short of legislation and thereby allowed her country to enhance its reputation both as a democracy and as a place where independence still exists. How well I recall our protest at the opening ceremony in the Lenin Stadium. Instead of an excited band of competitors following the flag around the track, there was British Olympic Association secretary Dick Palmer marching, dignified and alone, around the track. That statement meant more to onlookers, the Communists as well as the rest of us, than all the boycotts and political axe-grinding. The Games to me represent world peace, a unity of human beings far more persuasive than, for example, the United Nations. It doesn't matter what your race, colour or creed is. If you have watched, as I have, nation following nation at the closing ceremonies, ethnic groups with very recognisable different physical characteristics close together for only alphabetical reasons – Japan after Jamaica, for instance – then it brings home to you the meaning of the Olympic family. And as for the famous British aloofness, it has always been my experience that we have the happiest, most outgoing bunch of any. Who danced best and longest in Los Angeles?

Moscow was a far cry from that celebration. Overall the atmosphere was typically Communist and I think most people will understand what I mean by that: austere, regimented, with armed forces everywhere. Outside the athletes' village, soldiers patrolled with rifles while overhead helicopters churned up the sky. You were unwise to stray very far and, although the authorities tried to brighten our lives with discos and films, the general feeling was one of tedium. Neither did it pay to play practical jokes. One very silly competitor jumped out of a bush in front of our coach and without hesitation the guards on our bus were outside and waving guns at him. He could so easily have been shot. All the time we were being watched – an ATV engineer told me that when he and his friend went back to their hotel room one night they decided to search for the bug, which in this case was one of the listening devices that are installed, like taps or lights, in every room. After a few minutes, he turned to his pal and said that he knew where it would be – in the back of their television. So he took out a screwdriver and just as he was about to investigate, the 'phone rang. 'Will you please stop interfering with the television?' said a voice at the other end of the line. Very scary indeed.

Two unrelated incidents occurred the day before the qualifying round of my competition. As is my practice before big meetings, I travelled to the scene of my event the day before in an attempt to become familiar with the surroundings and settle down those nerves which affect practically all of us. Yet my visit to the Lenin Stadium filled me with dread. The place reminded me of a huge coffin, cold, impersonal and very much the end of the road. In sport, having the right buzz of adrenalin can be crucial, and here I was, very much aware of my own moods, on a downer. Wilf was unable to change the feeling of doom that had overtaken me. I was very fit, mentally alert and yet felt alone and anxious. I was expected to be the girl who could bring back gold or die in the attempt. Well, it was only the qualifying round and I knew I could throw 60 metres off a steady trot. Once through to the final, I thought, the adrenalin would soon be pulsing through me.

Back home in the West Midlands, my weights coach Brian Newman received a 'phone call from a friend of ours to say that he was sad I had failed to qualify. Brian shrugged off the remark, as anyone would, saying that the caller was bloody clever as the first round was not due until the next morning. No, the friend insisted, Tessa threw under 50 metres and is out of the competition. Brian took little notice except to ask how the chap knew this. A woman from Sycamore Road, Walsall, told me all the details, he said. Next day, the whole tale became true and Brian, listening to the news on the radio, could scarcely believe his ears.

Mary Peters, our team manager, had woken me at about seven o'clock. I felt twinges of apprehension – nothing unusual in that, they come all the time – and I didn't even wonder whether I was a little more scared than I should have been. Mary whispered, with the soft insistence that conceals a will of stainless steel, 'It's time, love', and for some reason it was like the final awakening before the death sentence is carried out. I was, to say the least, a little short on positive thinking. Four hours later I was on the runway for my first throw. I ran in, stopped and had another go. I was not coming in at all well and allowed my arm to fall far too low so that my hip dragged and I could not seem to pull it round. The javelin grudgingly failed to make even 50 metres, dropping almost flat to the turf. Not to worry, I thought, and that made matters worse. I was growing tense and I was not concentrating. Normally, I see and hear nothing; I might make encouraging noises and even smile – they are external exhibitions, inside there is only willpower. In Moscow, on a fearsomely hot morning, I began to fracture before thousands of people who could see no more than a black girl flunking her easiest examination. The next time I stepped over the line for a foul throw – shades of Christchurch – and suddenly I had only one trial left and my mind was in turmoil. 'This isn't happening to me', I thought. 'I'm the girl who doesn't let people down'. I tried, how I tried, but the moment my third throw left my hand I knew it was bad. It failed to make a mark and there I was – out, and with nowhere to hide. Head in hands, I screamed 'Oh! No!' and there were no tears that time, only anger and humiliation. I stormed from the arena into the tunnel and heard Andy Norman say 'Oh shit, she hasn't qualified!'. It was then that I discovered the loneliest place in the world, in front of a television camera with nothing to say except 'sorry'. Two television reporters, I can't remember who they were, stuck microphones under my nose and asked me how I was feeling. If I had been Daley, I would have said: 'Wonderful, thank you. I bust myself for four years for this. I've lost the man I loved, and today I failed even to qualify. Yes, I feel wonderful'. As it was, when Stuart Storey came up to me and put his arm around my shoulders, this girl at last just cried and cried and cried. I wanted to tear my heart out. 'Why did it happen to me, God? Why not someone else?'.

The news that the future world champion, Tiina Lillak, had also missed qualifying, along with Fatima and eventual world record-breaker Sofia Sakorafa, was of no interest at the time. I could not find Wilf so I went back to my room where Joslyn Hoyte and Sonia tried to console me. By then anger had turned to sullen desperation. I have never felt so beaten; beaten into the ground. That night Wilf admitted to me that he had left the stadium in a trance and had walked and walked for hours trying to come to terms with my failure. The truth was that mentally I had bombed out. I just hadn't the experience to keep myself composed. That night I wrote in my diary: 'Today is the loneliest day of my life'. There was to be one even lonelier. I did not want to wake up next day; to face the press, to meet people who would try to be kind when I knew I had let them down. I wanted to be by myself, to work things out; most of all I wanted to be with my Mum. I rang her and she said that when an ITV reporter told her I had not reached the final she had said 'You're joking' and had started to cry.

The pain inside took a while to seep away. It nagged me during the remainder of our stay in Moscow although I am not one of those people who go on and on about such things. Tomorrow really is another day. So I enjoyed watching Steve Ovett win the 800 metres and I sensed that Seb would come back in the 1500 metres – there is an awful lot of pride in that gentleman. For Daley, I felt even more. He was spectacular in winning Britain's first-ever decathlon gold medal and the picture of him, sweaty and triumphant, waving the Union flag remains as vivid to me as I know it does to his Aunty Doreen who was out there cheering with the rest of us. Wilf filmed the javelin final, with me appearing as the invisible woman and Maria Colon surprising us all by throwing 67.40 with her first effort and knocking Fuchs and the rest sideways. The Cuban girl was no better than sixth longest thrower as she went into the final, a massive long shot to Fuchs' near-certain victory. Colon has faded since then but at least she is still seen around the circuit. Fuchs is not. She was retired with inglorious haste, which only emphasises the difference between the East German system and ours.

As the day of our return neared, I began to wonder about the reception I would receive. There would be no parties, that much was certain. Mum gave me a hug and life went on as before; the Press reacted rather differently. How could a 69-metre thrower manage only 48 metres was the general drift. It was a question neither they nor I could ignore. I just did not need reminding of it as often as they seemed to think I did – I believe I could have had a nervous breakdown if I had not controlled my emotions. It was these that required attention and so I chose not to stay very long with my marvellous family but to go home to my empty flat and work things out for myself. I sat and wept for a while and then set off for Los Angeles 1984, armed with the first letter I opened on my return. It was from a nine-year-old girl and ended: 'Don't worry, you'll be all right next time'.

It was vital that I retained a goal. That thought kept me going not only through a defeat that quickly became one of history's unfortunate wee footnotes but also through three years of terrible misfortune. Among the mail that included the little girl's morale-booster were letters of hate, several of them from racists whose disgusting comments revealed only their own inadequacies, physical and mental. They are beneath contempt, these people, and today I know that our best weapon is to laugh at them. When you are down, however, cranks and head-cases are about the last thing you need. I much prefer to think of the way I was greeted at the Crystal Palace Coca-Cola meeting. I realised that it was important not to hide away and, rather as the air force sends crash pilots back into the air as soon as possible, I decided that I had to get that javelin airborne again. I was extremely nervous when I walked out to the centre of the field and there was still a hangover from Moscow because I could manage only third place with a modest 60.08 metres. Nevertheless, I was back in business and I was shaking with emotion as I stood on the podium. There were shouts of 'Lovely to see you, Tessa', 'Tessa, we love you' and 'Great to have you back' when I walked beside the crowd in front of the long-jump run-up. It was heart-rending. I really thought that people had dumped me. I am often surprised by how kind others are, just as the ability of some to be cruel leaves me equally shocked. Some said afterwards that I remained the people's champion. I hope that is true.

One last competition, the WAAA at Crystal Palace which I won with an encouraging 64.08 metres, and it was back to work at

Telford for a short time at least. The Development Corporation was winding up and this meant that I was to become unemployed at exactly the time when I most needed a regular job because the Variety Club members' sponsorship was now finished. I was a Commonwealth champion on the dole. At least I collected the dole money, when I wasn't too embarrassed because people recognised me. I used to sneak in and out only to be spotted and asked for my autograph. That seemed funny but I met some interesting kids, chatted with Rastafarians and enjoyed listening to the queuers. I never under-estimate people just because they are going through hard times, especially as often they are not responsible for being out of work. Four months after losing my job I joined two footballers, George Berry and Bob Hazell, who were then playing for Wolverhampton Wanderers, in a venture right next to the town's police station. The pair of them were great characters and they believed a plush leisure centre with me doing fitness classes was just what was needed in Wolverhampton. It may well have been but it didn't work out because neither had the experience to handle such a project and they had not really thought the business through.

Wilf and Brian helped me through some bad times over these months. Brian is a stoic Black Country type who takes life calmly whereas Wilf wants to take immediate action to rectify whatever he feels is wrong – and sometimes when it is pretty well right, too. Even so, their verdicts on Moscow were similar: inexperience in overcoming a situation I had not encountered before. They also insisted that I should go straight back into fight again. Wilf parted company from his employers, too, although the circumstances were very different. He had a disagreement over the low-level coaching structure and resigned from the British Athletics Board with whom he now maintains only the most rudimentary links, a fact that has had an adverse effect on my own career. Wilf became a lecturer at Leeds Polytechnic and it was therefore much more difficult to arrange our sessions; either he had to pay his own fares to and from Telford or I travelled to Leeds to stay with him and his family. This second option would have been the simpler except that within a week of my return from Russia, Unigate withdrew their sponsorship of me and demanded the return of the car they had provided. Wilf put it succinctly: 'In their eyes, Tessa, you have failed and the sad truth of this world is that no one really wishes to back a failure'.

The story, we knew, had to be re-written. At times like these, we all search for consolation. It came to me in the words of that nine-year-old girl and in the completed version of the little tale of Brian's friend and the woman with a gift of premonition. What I did not say earlier was that she had added: 'Tell her it will be all right next time'.

CHAPTER FIVE

Through Other Eyes

It is tempting, and easy, to sit in judgement of others. Obviously there are times, and writing a book is just such a time, when opinions must be hardened and choices made, based on facts, comments and relationships. When I was first approached to put my life on paper, I felt it would interest readers to discover what a close friend thought of me, to paint the portrait from another angle. I asked Wilf Paish to do this because he knows me in most of my moods and while he is a friend and colleague he also has to act as a guide and teacher. Throughout my career, and especially after Moscow, I have needed true friends but also people who could be a little objective. This, unexpurgated, is how Wilf sees me:

'Tessa is a woman of infinite variety. To say that she has moods could convey the wrong impression; but her face readily reflects her state of mind particularly to one who must rely on such visual expressions to conduct the subtle interchange of conversation. This is necessary for a coach before and during every training and competition session.

'When Tessa is happy her face reveals the true beauty which the good Lord gave her. The sparkling white of the eyes, the beaming smile revealing an array of cared-for ivory teeth, contrasting so magnificently with the polished ebony skin. In such a mood, Tessa is a charmer – she could even persuade the renowned Scot "to dip into his sporran" and part with a few bawbies. Fortunately these are frequent and oh, so different to those moods she turns on to order when confronted by the media. In her happy mood, Tessa is a coach's dream, a delight to work with, easy to motivate, sparkling in her performance. A session with Tessa then recharges the coach's batteries, makes up for all the heartbreaking sessions of the past and

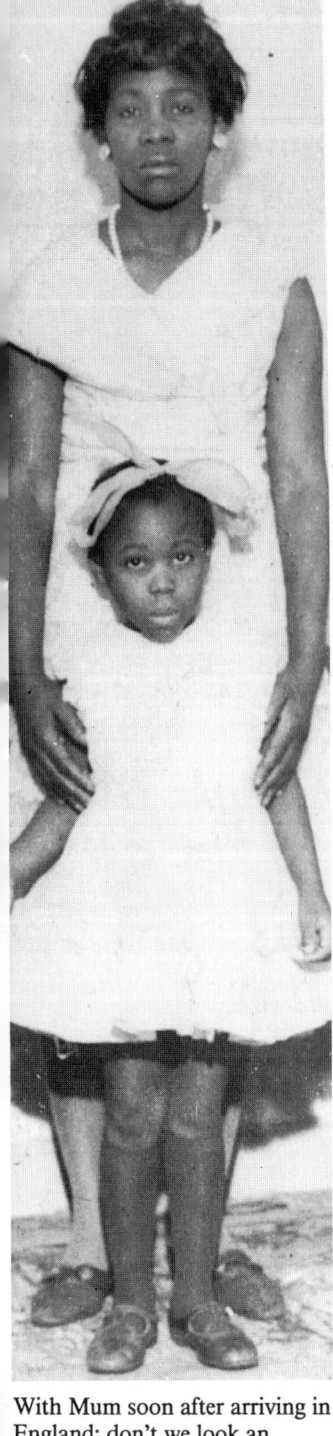

With my Grandmother in Jamaica in 1978. I didn't recognise her at first

With Mum soon after arriving in England; don't we look an anxious pair!

Airborne as a 15-year-old doing the long jump at Wards Bridge High School, which was one of my best events as a teenager

Above A shy look in Jamaica in 1978 while Edwin Moses stays as cool as ever. We are still good friends

Left Snapped with Wilf Paish before competing in the Lenin Stadium, Moscow in 1980, which was the scene of such calamity for me. This was my only recorded smile there

Seb, Sanderson and 'Smiler' at an Athlete of the Year presentation – just a couple of boyfriends I brought along

Dad, Mum and the proud bearer of the MBE. Everyone was solemn except me

Outside Buckingham Palace. Sonia Lannaman and me with the Sybil Abraham Award. Marea Hartman looks pleased. They are two ladies I respect and admire, despite Marea's outburst

Left Joining Mary Peters under canvas during a special Belfast youth week in 1985. No gold medals for camping technique here

Below Celebrating with friends in Leeds soon after Los Angeles. Clement is on my right

Princess Anne presenting me with the Sportswoman of the Year trophy in 1984. We nattered throughout dinner

those that will inevitably occur in the future. An experienced coach learns to detect this mood, takes advantage of it, and helps communicate it to his other athletes. It is the only reward the coach is likely to get or even expects – this is a labour of love and what better partner to share it with than Tessa.

'For me, the extremes of her moods, too, are instantly recognisable. When the glittering smile is absent, the eyes dull, almost unhappy, and the skin loses its sheen and has the pallor of matt-black I must play the father figure, for the drive of the extrovert motivator has no place. What better arena to learn the psychology of sport – books cannot explain the symptoms or remedies. It is all part of the treasured bond between athlete and coach working together towards a common goal, the result of experience. Those who wish to learn it can do so only by involvement. The path is a rough one to tread but the non-material rewards are worth the journey.

'These sessions always prompt the question "What's the matter?". The reply is equally predictable: "Nothing. I'm all right". "OK, let's warm up." Then the secrets are revealed. Sometimes it has been a boyfriend problem, or crazy anonymous 'phone callers disturbing her sleep. Small issues at work frequently play on Tessa's mind and become magnified into near-national disasters. But the commonest, and most difficult problem to resolve, seems to be the insensitive media who have portrayed Tessa, or her rivals, in terms she finds hard to accept. But once her feelings have been voiced, training proceeds unhindered, requiring a different motivational technique. One I frequently use is to offer her a competitive challenge. Even in this mood, Tessa is a competitor: she hates being beaten even at javelin target practice, blackjack or scrabble.

'Between these extremes comes the fascinating variety of moods, a psychologist's dream, an ever-changing pattern of communication that certainly makes Tessa different. I think she is at her best when surrounded by young people. If ever there was a natural pedagogue, Tessa is it. To take her into a school is an invitation for a re-enactment of the Pied Piper. Her bubbly personality rapidly makes the youngsters feel at home. This instant rapport would be envied by those who have spent a lifetime in teaching trying to achieve just that. She conveys the feeling of deep interest in each and every child and they just gaze at her or struggle to attract her attention to their recent works of art, spelling tests or literary contributions.

'With the Press, radio or television, there is this same natural, unspoiled quality. The good interviewer lets the sessions take their own course as Tessa, in her own articulate style, uses simple words supplemented by revealing facial expressions that often prompt the interviewer at the end to say: "What a girl!".'. Sitting in the press area at Los Angeles, surrounded by people who didn't know me from Adam, with the extra disguise of a deep sun-tan and a Spanish accreditation card around my neck, it was a delight to hear an American reporter say: "Gee, you should interview this Sanderson girl, she has some gems – and a good looker at that".

'Tessa has natural dress sense and is enough of an actress to turn up in the right creation for the right function in time to make the right impact. After her sport, clothes are probably her first love. She chooses them with care, thinks of the right match, especially the shoes – although the latter should never present a problem as she seems to have more pairs than the average shoe shop. Her ability in the clothing department, as in her throwing, far outstrips that of her rivals and training partners. Our Carnegie Hall training group was invited to a special dinner, one at which I felt it was important to make an impression. The men looked tidy, the girls neat enough. Tessa timed her entrance majestically, almost as if it were stage-managed, about three minutes to countdown and with all the others assembled: she was wearing just a simple off-white blouse, matching pleated skirt and white, high-heeled shoes. Had it been an interview for a job the others would have been out of work from that moment. Her appearance provoked the comment from out host: "You look smart". Her reply was "Do I?". Perhaps, like athletic ability, dress sense is an endowed characteristic which either you have or you haven't.

'While Tessa has a very strong will of her own, at times she is easily influenced by others. Frequently this creates a turmoil, particularly when she is presented with conflicting ideas from people she respects. In this situation she is sensitive and hates to hurt anyone's feelings: frequently I find myself apologising on her behalf when she finds she cannot resolve the conflict the situation has created.

'Tessa conveys a wonderful naïve quality with respect to her sport. While she recognises the stars and appreciates their performances, detailed statistics and history have little place in her world. Indeed, this very lack of knowledge can help her as such information on rivals often brings added pressure. Tessa's attitude is "let me throw it a long way, let my rivals worry about how far". And as far as she is concerned training and technique are the coach's worries, leaving her own mind clear to concentrate on her own performance. While it is not everyone's approach, it certainly suits Tessa's temperament. Like most other truly feminine women, Tessa has an obsession for anything that will enhance her natural beauty, that will make her look good and hence feel good. Had she saved what she has spent on clothes, she would be considerably better off. One day she came back from a visit to Maurice's family in Liverpool, ready to train but a trifle more bubbly than usual. "Guess what?" she said. In this situation there are 1,001 possibilities and I never prolong what she is itching to tell me. "I've just bought a fur coat – don't know how I could afford it but I just had to have it." I think the coat cost about £600, which probably rates at a pro rata of £60 per wearing. She is extremely generous with her clothes and frequently gives them away to friends and relatives, making an exception, I think, of the fur coat which remains somewhere in the back of her wardrobe.

'Her immaculate presentation of herself collapsed only once – and this is only my own personal observation – when she had her hair braided and beaded. It was then a new creation so far as I was concerned, and I did not like it. However, Tessa was bound to give it up when others followed the trend because she has no wish to be part of an identifiable group or set. She has to be a little bit different. Her usual style these days is to keep her hair short, retain the natural curl and highlight its quality with an oil that gleams and reflects the rays of the light.

'Tessa likes to be with boys and in the company of men. Frequently men make a carefree pass at her, particularly at promotional functions. In such a situation Tessa is an artist. One might almost suggest she is flirting with disaster, egging on her admirers, kidding them that there might just be a chance of an affair. Such episodes are nearly always brought to an abrupt ending. "Cheerio, I'm booking", she says and without hesitation she disappears to the sanctuary of her room or waiting car. Her advantage is that she has never acquired a taste for alcohol, while in most of these situations her admirers are the worse for wear on a meal with wine or an evening on cocktails. During the time I have known Tessa I could count on the fingers of one hand the number of times she has accepted an alcoholic drink, her favourite being squash or mineral water.

'She has, of course, had boyfriends and been involved in three affairs that could positively be called romances. Tessa is clever though in avoiding athletes in the teams, showing genuine affection for few, among whom were Brian Hooper and Edwin Moses. Contrary to the depiction of Sunday newspapers, athletics is not a sex-ridden sport, and recent developments make it less likely that it ever will be. In the past programmes finished with a formal banquet and ball after which there was lots of banter and whispered talk and, finally, the inevitable pairing-off. We are now, however, in the age of the young rebel and the banquets have disappeared completely, probably because of cost. Sometimes there is a low-key presentation meal but the favourite among athletes is a disco, for which jeans have superseded the ballgown. If one adds to this the great and increasing pressure placed on athletes, who often must step off one aircraft, compete, and then board another to the next venue, then the whole scene becomes thoroughly unromantic and each person merely a cog in a big, so-far successful business, the bubble of which must surely burst soon. Tessa's standards, including her moral ones and her expectations of men, must present a daunting doubt in the mind of any would-be suitor. Indeed, one might even say Tessa is looking for an old-fashioned boyfriend, a man who shows total respect accompanied by love and complete consideration. This is a rare breed now that coarseness appears to have taken over from courteousness as a manly quality. So her affairs of the heart are not without incident.

'Most of all, Tessa loves to be in a group. She readily makes friends and friendships are cherished as long as her own personal standards are not breached. Indeed, at a recent celebration in her honour, I was fascinated to see how much more at home she was with her regular training partners than with all the revered guests. The tell-tale remark "What's the gossip, girl?" did my heart good. It made me realise the gold medal razzmatazz will not change our Tessa. At her places of work, she forges strong bonds with her workmates, and once I had to cut a training session because she had to go to cheer her team, Guardian Royal Exchange, at a rounders match. On another occasion, the interlude between Tessa putting away the javelin and slamming a rounders ball all around the arena was less than 30 minutes. Her team won and the only person to run fully around the bases was, as if you couldn't have guessed, the ebony javelin-thrower. Yes, the group is important to Tessa, and her friends are as loyal to her as she is to them.

'Basically, she is a religious, family girl who from time to time really misses her Mum. By religious, I do not mean she is devout, but rather a good, practising Christian. She goes to church spasmodically but prays almost daily and is convinced that the Lord did not intend her to win in Moscow but really answered her prayers in Los Angeles. Amid the thousands of letters from well-wishers she received after the Games she singled out one to show me, saying "Isn't that nice, I'm going to do that". It was from a churchgoer who asked her to read a lesson from the Bible on Christmas Day.

'While Tessa now lives in Leeds, she retains indissoluble family ties. She is always making references to her mother and when she is really low – and this happens from time to time – she either 'phones her Mum in Wood End or makes a fleeting visit to see her. She is constantly worrying about her parents' finances and is always prepared to share her money with them. About a month before Los Angeles, with her own personal account well and truly in the red, she made efforts to find some money to help her brothers reform a pop

61

group. And in London, with the choice of top hotels at her beckoning, you will often find her staying with her sister or her Aunty Kitty.

'Tessa is fastidious about cleanliness. From time to time we have been housed in dingy hotels in foreign countries. While most of the team accept the situation as part of the sport and Tessa usually goes along with the group, I can always recognise the uneasy feeling in her: for some reason she feels she has been let down. On such trips, she is only truly happy when she has a single room where she can have complete privacy when she needs it. Often, of course, a single room for each member of the team is an impossibility and on many occasions I have tried to anticipate problems by suggesting suitable rooming partners, who are other female athletes, in a quiet word with the team management. This was never difficult with under-standing types such as Mary Peters or Pam Piercy, the ex-athlete manager who rightly has been used in the more recent era. Others have been less sympathetic and refused to change a scheduled rooming list only to produce an unhappy, and less efficient, competitor. Some might say this is part of Tessa's selfishness – it isn't. Indeed she is, in many respects, one of the most unselfish people I have met. It is just a part of the self-imposed standards which govern her life and she isn't good at compromising herself.

'I consider myself fortunate in having shared Tessa's sorrows and triumphs, from the unhappy and tearful episode of Moscow to the joyous, yet still tearful chronicle of Los Angeles.'

Those are Wilf's views, some of which I disagree with but all of which I respect because of what we have shared. He has been loyal, sincere and, although there are times when I think he takes on far too many burdens, spreading himself too thinly across his many athletes, he is so conscientious that it would be unjust to complain too strongly.

As the first year of the decade melted into the second, so we decided that I must have a new challenge to help me expand and then, with luck, fulfil my talents. The natural step for an all-round athlete was to take on the heptathlon, particularly as the extension of the pentathlon from five events had led to the inclusion of the most testing of them all, the javelin. I knew that unless I threw as I had in Moscow, I would more than make up in my speciality for what I lost in the 800 metres, which is to me what the 1500 metres is to Daley Thompson – a delayed explosion that never occurs. First of all, however, I embarked on another of Andy Norman's trips to Australasia. We certainly earned our fares on this one, hopping from Auckland to Wellington and then Christchurch in New Zealand before travelling to Melbourne and Sydney in Australia, all in 15 days.

The last trip had been fun, even if I had been distressed by the break with Maurice. This one was hard work. We met David Moorcroft in New Zealand, a country he wisely wintered in each year, for of all the Commonwealth lands this is very special both in its somewhat genteel, old-world appeal and in its magnificent settings. The Australians are, well, just Australian – a breed apart. They bite. I won all my competitions in New Zealand, one of them with 63.72 metres and was second twice in Australia.

Wilf and I decided I should split the season, concentrating domestically on the heptathlon, internationally on the javelin. I loved the mixture. Having thrown 65.32 metres in early May in Birmingham, I went back a week later to compete in my first seven-eventer, the Midland championships, in which I came second to Judy Livermore, totalling 5,841. My high-jump, at 1.60 metres, was terrible but the javelin and sprints pushed me very close to Judy, who I believe has never fully used her own, immense resources. My second try was an international with Canada in Saskatoon, a meeting at which Daley Thompson planned an assault on the world decathlon record. The weather was so bad, however – lashing rain and a cold wind – that he gave up after the first day's five events and acted as a cheerleader for me. What a joker he can be! As we lined up for the final event, the much-hated 800 metres, I knew even a very modest time would secure the Commonwealth record. I had completed an excellent 100 metres hurdles in 13.76 seconds, putt the shot and high-jumped well enough to create personal bests and even to make up for my average performances in the 200 metres, javelin and long-jump: now I needed to batter my way through that prairie wind for two laps. Down the final straight, I was dying but there were Daley, Colin Boreham and Pan Zanue behind the finishing line, urging me to keep my legs flailing. Closer and closer I came to the tape and now Daley had his arms wide apart to catch me as I fell. I flung myself forwards at him – and he sidestepped. I landed face downwards in thick mud, down to earth from my record-breaking performance. He just stood there, the devil, laughing. Then he helped me up and gave me a hug. I had beaten Judy by 140 points, scoring 5,906.

Now I had the heptathlon in my blood. Images of Mary Peters and her great Munich success were gradually coming into focus. Wilf really believed I was a potential world record-breaker and, I must say, so did I. Hadn't I, after all, broken the record without doing more than my usual winter training for the javelin? Wouldn't I have done even better in Canada if my tendon had not been sore? My next and maybe last heptathlon was the high point of my whole career. It took place at a European Cup semi-final in Brussels where I was placed second behind Sabine Everts, breaking the Common-wealth record for the second time in two meetings. Despite personal bests in the hurdles (13.72 seconds) and the 200 metres (24.89 seconds) I was eighth overnight before a best-ever long-jump of 5.97 metres and then a javelin throw of 64.64 metres – still a world record in the heptathlon and in this case the earner of 1,105 points which brought me to within 6 of Everts, who is from West Germany. As usual, the 800 metres exhausted me and my 2 minutes 26.20 seconds was nearly 18 seconds slower than Everts, allowing her to win comfortably with 6,350 points. Multi-event expert Alan Lindop reported: 'What score will she amass when she trains seriously for the heptathlon, one wonders'. I am still wondering, for I am sure I could appreciably cut my hurdles and 800-metre times, improve my shot to around 14 metres and high-jump and long-jump better. Evidence to support this contention was provided at the WAAA championships on 25 July and I also had the unbeatable pleasure of giving Shirley Strong a nasty turn. Strongy is a good friend of mine, a girl and a half who, after some early mutual suspicion, became a confidante and pal. Her outrageous sense of humour has brightened many a day – and night. She is very serious about her event though, smoking heavily as a pre-race nerve-settler. On this occasion, I took off from the start and by the eighth of the ten hurdles still led the British record-holder (13.06 seconds at the time). It was then that the specialist training told in her favour, for she summoned up all her strength and edged past me to chest the line inches clear. Maybe I need a bigger chest. She looked at me with a puzzled expression and I broke into a giggle. 'I nearly had you there, Strongy', I joked, and she nodded in agreement, then joined in the laughter. My time was 13.46 seconds, still a personal record.

It was an excellent year for me in the javelin, too, and I was persuaded that I could at least in part make up for my Moscow misery by retaining the Commonwealth championship and, a good deal tougher assignment, improve by one place on my European silver. I was beaten just once in the season, by an Eastern Bloc shooting star, Antoenata Todorova who, at just 18 years old, broke the world record with 71.88 metres to my 65.94 metres in the European Cup final in Zagreb. I was not very happy about that for two reasons: I had beaten her in the European semi-final six weeks earlier and my confidence at this time had me hoping that the world best was within my reach. Not much has been heard of Todorova since she went to the World Cup in Rome as European representative.

Earlier, at Furth, I had increased the second best throw of my life to 68.86 metres and then beat Fatima at Crystal Palace, although not by much. I was 1.10 metres ahead of her 64.18 and I knew for certain that Sanderson versus Whitbread was going to be a long-lasting fixture. Twice later on, I threw beyond 68 metres but the best effort of the year was reserved for a field in Spalding, Lincolnshire, where at the request of shot-putter Geoff Capes I hurled the javelin 67.24 metres with the wind in the wrong direction. Six months later, my life had gone in the wrong direction, too.

CHAPTER SIX

Limping Along

Every competitor suffers a setback at one time or another. The nature of athletics is to test physical fitness to the maximum point, and when that point is overreached, as it invariably is, something goes bang. Of all the Olympic athletic gold-medal winners of my generation, only Daley Thompson has avoided a lengthy spell of convalescence and that may be because he does not compete very often. Seb Coe, Steve Ovett and Allan Wells have suffered seriously and not necessarily with fibre injuries, for Coe and Ovett were both absent for long periods through viral conditions. Indeed, I often wonder whether the supremely fit are not specially susceptible to that kind of attack; no doubt there are learned articles on such matters. My setback was horrifyingly simple and yet I am convinced that it had two permanent effects on me, one of them bad, the other good. On the minus side, I believe that I would have been a heptathlete of the highest order, perhaps a world-record breaker, maybe a world or Olympic champion – certainly records have gone to scores that I know I could have beaten and, equally, the Los Angeles gold medal was gained by Glynis Nunn, of Australia, with a score that I am tempted to call modest. That is not fair comment, I realise, because Glynis beat the opposition on the day just as I did in the javelin, but event by event her totals were more than attainable and would have been humbled had Ramona Neubert or any two or three East Germans been at the Memorial Coloseum. No wonder Judy Livermore was so upset at coming fifth. I understand that she and her marvellous coach John Anderson had angry scenes afterwards and if she made John – a wildly enthusiastic Scotsman who appreciates the athlete's burden – angry then things must have been very wrong. Judy ought to have won that gold. She has the

66

potential to be the female Daley Thompson. Now it may be too late.
I hope the end of her Birmingham Polytechnic studies will force her
to concentrate on exploiting her talent.

The positive side of serious injury is obvious. When – not if, that
is negative thinking – you overcome your problems you have a layer
of strength within you that, as Boy Scouts say, will help you
overcome all difficulties. It is the Muhammad Ali syndrome,
challenging fate and age and fatness and still coming out on top. Ali,
who was one of my great heroes, was unfortunately pushed too far
and when I met him I was very disappointed. From a distance I
loved what he was and much of what he stood for; there is little
question, however, that while he was becoming the most famous
man in the world he was also being ruthlessly exploited. Sports stars
have to be very cautious about whom they trust.

I was vibrantly fit in that winter of 1982, looking forward to
retaining my Commonwealth championship and proving, with a
European gold, that I was the best in the world. I was not concerned
that my left Achilles' tendon had niggled the season before and I was
training on 300-metres repetitions – a savage way to build in stamina
at speed – as well as with the normal weights and strength work
which had brought me a near 14-metre practice shot putt. I had a 6
March date with my club, Wolverhampton and Bilston, at Cosford
and was glad enough to break out of the routine to help my friends
in the national indoor relays. The programme was to run four races
in 90 minutes and having gone well in the qualifying round of the
4 × 400 metres, I rested and then sprinted my 100 metres in the
4 × 100 qualifier. It was after this that my leg began to tingle, like
pins and needles only more irritating. I went to the physiotherapist
and said that I had a terrible sensation in my lower leg, what was the
matter? He diagnosed a minor attack of tendonitis, strapped up the
ankle and said I would be all right. I was not convinced because I
could not put too much weight on my foot; however, I did not want
to let the team down in the finals and so I agreed to go ahead.
Anyone who has been to Cosford knows about the heavy camber on
the bends and it was as I was coming out of one into the straight,
overtaking a rival and moving into second overdrive, that I felt a

'ping!' at the back of my ankle. For an instant it did not seem much but suddenly I was up in the air, out of control, crash-landing on to the elbow of my throwing arm which cracked like a stick. Nausea overcame me as slowly I tried to rise, clutching my painful elbow. My shoulder was weeping blood from the friction burns and my vest hung sadly off my shoulder. A crowd surrounded me, concerned, but I just wanted to be alone and tried to stand up: there, to my horror, was my foot, dangling from my leg in some weird corruption of Bambi's first walk. I nearly fainted. The club doctor, Colin Brown, hurried over and thrust his thumb into the back of the Achilles. There was no tendon, no sinew, nothing, just a big hole – a complete rupture. It was Moscow with knobs on. My new world had collapsed under me, just like that tendon. As I was carried from the track I prayed 'Please, Lord, don't let it be too bad'.

It was. And to make matters worse there were, to put it politely, hospital complications. As Colin Brown drove me to Birmingham General Hospital, I worried about two little boys whom I had taken to Cosford to watch me compete. How were they going to get home? Then I was on a hospital stretcher and a nurse kept asking if I was all right and which leg was it. I don't recall much more until I awoke in bed, my arm in a bandage and my leg in a pot. After five days I was allowed out and within a short time the mobility in my ankles had impressed the physios so much that they thought I was ready to work on the joggers. I repeatedly told them: 'I'm not ready yet' but they were so persistent that in the end I complied. The result was terrible: the stitching tore apart. In fitness terms, the wasted time meant that I was back beyond even the pre-operative state and, perhaps, I was beginning to think, out of athletics forever.

The tendon was stitched back and this time the pot went over my leg for another three weeks. At first my sister had to wash me, although when the plaster came off my elbow I could at least manipulate my right arm sufficiently to pull my knickers on. I swear I needed size 50 to pull them over that potted ankle! Climbing up and down stairs was a terrible problem, too: I was loaded like a sack of coal on to the strongest back around and hauled up to my room. Maurice's family put me up for a while and, when I became rather frustrated at Wood End, I moved back to Telford where my friend Del Sanderson (no relation), Pat my sister and my family did a lot of my chores. With time on my hands, I seriously considered giving up athletics. After Moscow and then this, I was sure there was a jinx on me.

At times like these, you need sensible encouragement and wise counsel. And the moments I recalled later were the unexpected signs of affection and hope. On the morning after the accident, I was still dazed by anaesthetic when a telephone call was put through to my bedside. A nurse was on the line. 'And now I just need a joke', I thought as she said 'There's a Mr Coe for you'. Sure enough, it was Seb. I could hardly understand him but there was this warm, mellow voice saying that everyone was thinking of me and that I had to look after myself with the greatest care.

Once I had dismissed the mood of melancholy, I made plans with Wilf and Brian. What a godsend Brian was! His attitude was perfect. Devastated by Moscow, I made the utmost use of his advice, often given while we stood amid the sweating, straining bodies that packed the down-and-out Littleton Street premises with unremitting effort. It was his calm authority that helped me combat that first disappointment, unaware at the time that his wife, Pat, was being taunted with remarks about how Brian's girlfriend had flopped. Vicious tongues make light work of good reputation.

Brian rang me regularly before I went back to what training I could manage. He would say 'We'll start at the beginning and build you all the way up'. Then came the ego-boosting: 'I know I am dealing with someone exceptional and I am certain you will be back'. Then the warning which really was a masterpiece of psychology because it was Newman's Law of Challenge: 'If you can stand the things I am going to do, you can't fail'. His problem was that my body strength had wasted away as muscular development was lost. Laid up in Wolverhampton there was nothing I could do about that, though I did try a few useless little exercises. Brian emphasised that my body would tell me when I could return to the weights room. It was more than two months before it did. After Los Angeles, I asked him what his impressions were when I struggled back to the gymnasium. We could afford to chuckle – by then it was almost a pleasure to see what we had come through – when he said: 'You were a bloody cripple; couldn't even get into the squat position. We were back to worse than square one because after the first operation, you couldn't handle weights that a baby could lift. There was immobility in the limbs themselves. That tendon is the biggest in the body and it affected the mobility in your legs. You were in pain and that is no condition in which to lift weights. It can be positively dangerous. Anyway, you were not giving the muscles the physiotherapy they needed. So we both started with no weights at all, just exercises. Me, too. It would have done you no good to watch me using weights'.

Brian was most concerned about my ankles, for there were already tell-tale clues to a weakness in the right ankle as well. He bought a leg press machine to encourage flexibility, pushing the bar as high as it would go so that I was forced to stretch my heels. Then we began high squats, gradually lowering them until after three months I was able to knee-bend fully. He was a superb motivator, speaking almost confidentially of how I had improved, measuring it week by week, almost as if I was learning to walk again, which in a sense I was. Then another and longer-lasting problem appeared. It has been explained to me that the skin of black people does not knit so well as that of whites. The result of this can be killoids, huge water blisters that blow up over old stitching and then burst, weeping blood and fluid. There appears to be nothing to do but grin and bear it, and that is what I have to do to this day. I am constantly bandaging and padding the area but the treatment only eases the discomfort.

Cycling was another of my occupations, I would ride at least five miles a day on a bicycle which had generously been given to me. I don't remember who suggested that cycling would be good for me, but it was not anyone from the British Athletics Board, that much is certain. They were conspicuous by their silence, so all my rehabilitation work – and no doubt that of many another injured athlete – was done on the strength of freelance suggestion and the experiences of other people. How I envied footballers! At the best clubs, they had expert treatment for almost any form of injury and I am convinced that no star player would have been left to his own resources as I was by all but Brian and one or two others. I noticed that last year the Board appointed a doctor to oversee the inauguration of a medical structure for athletes, a step that underlined the non-material benefits of professionalism over amateurism. I think comments from Seb Coe and Steve Ovett embarrassed the Board to such a degree that they were forced to act.

The official contacts I had were from Marea Hartman, who said that if there was anything I required from the WAAA she would do her best to provide it, and from Frank Dick, national director of coaching. Oh yes, there was another one. It came from Margaret Whitbread, national javelin coach, who rang to invite me to compete against her daughter, Fatima, for cash. It was tactless to say the least. It was only my first week out of plaster. I was also very grateful to the Sports Aid Foundation who continued with their financial support at a time when I was so far into the red, I was marooned. But it was a hard, hard time. I had to decide whether or not to carry on and deep down it was a closer verdict than many might have thought. The strength to continue came from the people around me, like the mob at Littleton Street who, in between the grunts and the jesting, would tell me to 'stick in there, ower kid'. There was Sonia, too, Wendy Hoyte, Helen Barnett and buddies like Roy Mitchell and Wilbert Greaves. Wilf would not even contemplate the end of my career. How thankful I am for that.

I had one competition in 1982 and this, on the face of it, was a minor triumph. We now know it to have been a dreadful mistake and I can only believe that had I been medically advised, and intelligently cautioned by the Board, then it would never have happened. I was concerned to show them that I was still around, a force in reserve, readying myself to charge to the front again. For their part, they hinted that they wanted to know whether I could be expected to throw at the Commonwealth Games in Brisbane that October. On 28 August, I removed all the pressure of publicity in the time-honoured way of competing for my club at a minor meeting somewhere in the wilds. In this instance, I travelled on to

Coatbridge, Scotland, because Bob Roberts, Wolverhampton secretary and one of the kindest and most considerate of men, wanted my return also to help the women's team. It was the kind of gesture anyone would make for Bob, who died a couple of years ago to heartfelt mourning. My first throw flew exactly 66 metres, a distance that set me dancing with glee. Not for long though; the glee became a grimace, for by the time I had climbed into my car, an enormous killoid had formed. I could not put my shoe on. Now I knew that my insistence on competing had been madness, that I should have resisted the pressure which I had permitted to be put on me. Yes, when all was said and done, it was my fault: I could always have said 'no'. I was in great pain on the journey home but I stayed quiet about it, subconsciously I suppose hoping it would heal quickly and I could risk competing in Brisbane. However, it remained and eventually I had to have it cut away, leaving the skin even more tender than it had been, in some ways similar to the scar tissue that yields repeatedly over the eyes of a susceptible boxer. From then on, I knew that each competition would leave a bloody mess in my sock. I had to pretend that it wasn't bad. At least I had the satisfaction of knowing that I had thrown way over the Brisbane qualification distance.

When the team left I felt hollow inside. I had viewed the Games as a first chance to throw a spade of earth on the coffin of Moscow. It was then that I said firmly again to myself: '1984 is the time to do that, little sister'. I forced myself to be content that at least I was on my way.

Fatima took the bronze in Brisbane behind the Australian pair Sue Howland, a slightly surprising winner, and Petra Rivers. I am no great spectator or statistician, so my recollection of the European championships is that Fatima was sixth or so – a good result – and as she also threw 66.98 metres that year I was displaced from the top of the UK annual list for the first time since 1973. Anna Verouli won the European title with 70.02 metres in front of her home crowd in Athens. Since that victory she has been accused of taking anabolic steroids and I have to say that as a specimen of womanhood she is among the bulkiest and ugliest I have ever seen. Stupidly, she even thought she could fool the Olympic medical authorities and was hauled out of the games in Los Angeles when tests on her proved positive. She must have badly needed those drugs because had she stopped taking them a month or so earlier the chances would have been greatly against detection.

In 1983 Fatima established herself. She was as hungry for medals and recognition as I had been in 1978, believing that she could relegate me to number two in Britain and promote herself to number one in the world. Fine ambitions and, for me, exactly the spur I needed. We had never been especially friendly but I had, and retain, respect for her ability and the driving desire she has to look down from the top. I have it, too. We were to become the Coe and Ovett of women's athletics but, unlike those magnificent middle-distance men, there was no chance that either of us would wish to avoid competing against each other. We would have been happy to do so for a penny, let alone the millions once shunned by Seb and Steve.

By then I had moved to Leeds to be among the warm friendliness of the West Riding. Unable to find a job in the West Midlands, and with Wilf such an infuriating distance away, I packed my bags rather later than would have been the case had I not suffered the injuries, and was soon pleasantly settled in a one-bedroomed flat the council kindly found me. Within months, I had found not one job but two, the second of which, with a television promotion company called Telvista, was to last until just after Los Angeles. The company were terrific, allowing me time off to train as well as providing a car and a salary of £8,000 a year. The winter's training had been good for me. I needed a taste of competition, however, and quietly threw more than 64 metres in Acoteias, the camp sponsored by the International Athletes' Club at the Algarve, Portugal. I was nearing readiness for my first important event, the UK championships in Edinburgh on 28 May, when Fatima and I would be responding to each other's respective challenge.

It is always either raining or about to rain in fair Edinburgh and, true to form, the thin cold mist of water covered everything, making the runway so hazardous that I would rather have walked on my hands and knees down Princes Street than sprint up and stride wide to throw the javelin. I could not just withdraw, however, so I risked it. I do not mind admitting that I was scared to death and, as it happened, I was pleased to have thrown as far as I did with 61.44 metres to 62.14. I also took all six throws because, although I was in agony trying to hold my footing, I just could not afford to mentally duck out. I was fighting and had broken an important barrier by forcing my way back into competition. We met again in Birmingham a week later, ostensibly to beat the Russians, but we were not kidding each other about that. I was having to pump my foot with cortisone injections and the huge swelling from Meadowbank had only just subsided. I warmed up with meticulous care, heavy bandaging under my socks supporting both ankles. When I ran in I knew I could get up on my toes but I was also aware that I could not hold the balance. With all the nervous energy at my command I heaved into the throw and watched, amazed, as the javelin soared beyond 70 metres for the first time in my life. It was a UK all-comers and Commonwealth record of 70.82 and, with Fatima producing a personal best of 67.46 metres, the Russians were consigned to the minor placings. I was flying now and we returned to Edinburgh where on 26 June it was only about to rain although the weather was making up for this with wind. My first throw, as at the Alexander Stadium in Birmingham, was the boss, a massive surge forward to 73.68 metres, a mark that remains my best and at the time was the third longest in history behind Tiina Lillak's record 74.76 metres and Sofia Sakorafa's 74.20. It was epic stuff, anyway, and good, too, for Fatima who threw 68.36 metres. Perhaps I overdid the competition because my arm was giving me problems again and from then until the end of the season it repeatedly went numb. I was also advised that my Achilles' tendon was again in a poor state and that I would do better to miss Helsinki and the first world championships. There was never a chance of that.

In Finland, javelin-throwing is the national sport. Tiina Lillak, naturally enough, is a princess and anyone intending to prevent her ascension to the throne of the world championships in her own city, Helsinki, was in for a mighty skirmish. Fatima almost did and I admire her greatly for coming good at the right time. Me? I had two tasks in that fair city of pine and lakes: first, to qualify for the final; second, to complete the round. If I won a medal, that would be marvellous, but I was not about to put that kind of pressure on myself. Moscow taught me to take nothing for granted. The press harangued me for pre-competition interviews about my feelings before qualification. Was I tense? Yes. Confident? Yes. Would I go through to the final? Undoubtedly, yes. I had been failure's companion once before and on 12 August in Helsinki there was no way that I would slink out with him again. Let the devil find another. So I kept very calm and threw a couple of warm-up shots beyond the 60-metre qualifying mark. No shakes this time. Get in there, girl. And I threw an easy 64.80 metres. Meanwhile, Fatima was having problems which, creditably, she overcame with a third and last effort of 60.96 metres which put her through as the bottom marker of 12 finalists.

What did that matter? She took the event next day by the collar, stepping in to wham home an opening throw of 69.14 metres. The javelin is like that: unpredictable, it hands out its favours without rhyme or reason, save for the fact that generally a really long throw has a foundation of consistent good ones. After I threw the British record in Edinburgh, many pundits called it a fluke and I suppose that the fact that perfect wind conditions and technical precision coincided at a given instant made it something of a wonder. But you just never know. It was very nearly Fatima's night. In the Olympic stadium that warm evening the capacity crowd almost introduced new gravitational forces for their princess. The rest of us were almost bystanders as Tiina inched her way towards the target, closer and closer but seemingly fractionally out of reach as she moved in for her sixth and final throw. Then, the great competitor that she is, Lillak summoned up a flier that brought a concerted sigh from her supporters and, more to the point, a winning 70.82 metres. There was pandemonium, Tiina leaping about and charging around the track, arms aloft, laughing in triumph to a platoon of photographers – very understandable but unfair on rivals who had yet to throw. I tried to follow her and even went to the length of asking photographers to give me room for my attempt. I might as well have tried to stem the Baltic Sea for all the good it did. She was flying Finland's flag that evening and the whole nation had stopped to applaud her. I had to wait, and by then the adrenalin had dribbled away so that, flat in mind and flat of throw, I failed to improve and had to be content with fourth place behind Lillak, Whitbread and Verouli, whose fifth-round 65.72 beat my best, 64.76. By then, however, I was painfully aware that the killoid had formed and burst and that blood was oozing over my shoe.

I was tempted to feel self-pity. There was a six-inch rent in my heel, packed tight with scar tissue that wept through cracks as soon as the foot stretched. But after some thought I concluded with John Trower, my adviser over that period because Wilf, disappointingly, was coaching in Canada, that I had nothing to grumble about; fourth in the world after what I had been through was not to be sniffed at. Helsinki was important for much more than my own peace of mind because it was there that I became involved with Miklos Nemeth, the 1976 Olympic javelin champion from Hungary, who was to play a key role for me in the year left before Los Angeles. Miklos, whose huge presence is acknowledged and enjoyed on both sides of the Iron Curtain, was standing at the top of a flight of stairs deep in conversation with some of his discus-throwers. He suddenly stopped and dashed down to give me a hug. 'How are you, Tessa?', he asked. 'That was the best I have seen from you for ages. One problem. Your stride is too long and you're up and down on your toes, coming up but not holding the position.' I showed him the scar. There was the faintest pause, then he added: 'You are ready to win the next Olympics. I tell you that. You come to Hungary and train and you will win the next Olympics'. I thought how wonderful it was, two days after I had been defeated by 6 metres, that he should think that. Talk about motivation – if he thought I could win, why shouldn't I? He was the last person I would have expected to take that sort of interest.

Before I was ready to pit myself once more against Lillak, Petra Felke and others at the spearhead, there was some unfinished and distinctly worrying business. We had concluded – Wilf, Dr David

Durie, a Barnsley GP in whom we had the utmost confidence, and I – that we would take the advice of Tony Banks, a very experienced surgeon in sport, who recommended operations not only on the slow-healing tendon but on the other, too. This had been weakened by the stress placed on it through my favouring the injured leg and had meant that throughout the season it was only really possible to throw and run once a week. I had been most careful not to refer publicly to these problems because they might have sounded like excuses. Indeed, they still do, which is why it has always been my contention that a beaten competitor is silly to squeal. It does not touch the winner and only detracts from the loser's plausibility.

Ten days after the world championships I was, courtesy of the International Athletes' Club's excellent scheme through BUPA, undergoing surgery secretly in Bolton Hospital, Lancashire. There was no time to be lost. A few days away for a mishap here or an accident there could have put Los Angeles out of reach. It was then that Wilf and Brian – charts and programmes, schemes and ideas gelling –were indispensable. They knew what they wanted me to do and I was not about to let them down.

Others, too, had faith in me. Barry Whitford, director of Telvista, was the ideal employer, for he was aware that his company's requirement for publicity went hand in hand with full scope for my training. When he had asked me: 'Give me one good reason why I should employ you' I had replied 'Because I am going to win the gold medal in Los Angeles'. This displayed a confidence I did not always feel but it set the conditions for my employment, something I had not been able to arrange when I worked at Guardian Royal Exchange where a manageress was unwilling to understand the relationship between winning and training: the more you put in, the more you extract. Barry's personal secretary, Anita Daley, also impressed me with her poise and professionalism so it was here that I found at last a suitable environment for the combination of work and sport.

At Carnegie College, too, I merged into Wilf's gang, the senior lunatic among a crowd of them. Mick Makins, a triple jumper known therefore as **Mick the Jump, and Mick Hill, (Mick the**

Spear), a javelin-thrower of growing reputation, were my special pals. They quickly responded to my moods, listened to my troubles and then, almost as if they had pressed a switch, I would find myself being kidded along, laughing at their 'damned cheek' as I called it. Great lads. I have heard them reduce pomposity to absurdity in seconds – and their 'mooning' act has to be seen to be believed.

Both my legs were in plaster until just before Christmas and it was a major task to travel from the office to Carnegie College and back to fit in the body-work that remained vital. It is typical of Yorkshire people that any number offered to help me: in the end Gayle Ripley, an office colleague, blonde and sophisticated, turned out to be the most adept chauffeuse, opening doors and carrying my sandwiches. I wasn't at all surprised when she became a British Airways air stewardess – probably on the strength of my training!

Towards the end of my convalescence I was in Scotland when a friend rang to inform me that I had been omitted from the elite squad of athletes who were to be given special dispensations over qualifying for the Olympic Games. I was thunderstruck. Fatima and Kathy Cook were in, I was out: Britain's number one javelin-thrower, record-holder, fourth in the world championships. Was the country so richly endowed with field event competitors that the selectors could spurn me without a word? What had I done that they did not like? Did my face no longer fit? Had so much time and effort been put into Fatima that I was now a secondary item? Officially it was said that only athletes in a medal position in the world, European or Olympic Games, or world record-holders were considered elite. It was a diabolical decision and Wilf was darkly suspicious that it had had a good deal to do with his own fraught and bitter tangle with his former employers at the Board. He had to re-plan my schedule around a meeting or two at which I would have to prove myself to the Board. That did not create too many problems. What intensified his anger was the fact that he took three of his other Olympic contenders, Peter Elliott, Steve Sole and Sue Morley, to Crystal Palace for a meeting on their plans and nothing came of them. As far as I was concerned, not a single request for a competition abroad, away from domestic rivals, came to anything.

Only Andy Norman's entrepreneurial skills in the end came to my rescue. Whatever I may say about him later, I am eternally grateful that he at least raised his sights above factional jealousies. The rejection of my elite status brought a single-minded response. As I said to Wilf, 'I am going to work my butt off to spite those sons of bitches'.

So work I did, but it was not until February 1984 that I was deeply, exhaustingly involved. Over Christmas at Wood End Road, Mum looked with concern at the ankle which continued to weep. I was walking by then, impatient but aware of the dangers of doing too much too soon. Brian was re-teaching me for the second time how to squat, for I had not only lost mobility but a quantity of muscle, too, no less than $1\frac{1}{2}$ inches around the calf. The Raleigh bicycle was also back in use around the streets of Wednesfield. By February I was jogging and striding – six months to J-Day and every yard a step in the right direction – and I was feeling better every day, except for a ten-minute spell each morning when I could not get my legs out of bed they were so stiff and painful around the tendons. They were not strong yet but I was assured by Dr Banks that they would not rip. The two Micks were working with me at Carnegie even though often they had to slow down. We regarded ourselves as the Black and White Minstrel Show, always cackling at some rude joke or jostling together. Mick the Spear is an aggressive worker, too, and liked me to advise him on technical bits and pieces. With Wilf's blessing, because he could see the benefit of a second opinion, it was in March that I accepted Miklos Nemeth's invitation and trained in Hungary for two weeks. The place, Tata, not far from Budapest, was bleak and the national Hungarian training camp looked more like an army barracks. No chance of skiving here. This was a place of work and wasn't I to find out how! Boy was it tough. I had only just re-started stamina work and so training hard twice a day left me breathing hot embers while my stomach cramped up from the sit-ups and specially-designed medicine ball routines. I was so tired I thought my body would pack up like an old, used car. Yet it was also an addiction because it squeezed everything else from my mind. I returned in April, June and July for further running repairs.

It was to be a vicious blow for Miklos when the Soviet Union forced Hungary to pull out of the Los Angeles Games. For the athletes it was even worse. He at least had competed previously and, anyway, was allowed to travel freely while they, poor people, were locked in without a key. For a Communist Bloc country, Hungary is not tightly controlled and there is plenty to buy and see. At the Nemeths' home where Miklos's children study English I had dinner several times, causing a stir around his neighbourhood where a black was, I fancy, not so much unusual as previously unseen. I was subject to a lot of curious stares, which reminded me of the time that Wendy Hoyte, a little joker if ever there was one, Sonia and a few of us were in Dresden, East Germany. We were going into our hotel when Wendy started to pose in front of a growing crowd. She said: 'Tessa, they're watching me because they've never seen a black person before'. We started giggling until an East German walked over and explained in perfect English: 'May I assure you, young lady, that we have'. Wendy's face dropped to her navel.

Miklos has been through all the emotional ups and downs himself and, although my debt to Wilf is great, he will admit himself that top competitors communicate on a different plane. They know what it is like to be one down and two to play, the very essence of sporting battle, and they know from instinct when an athlete is not putting in quite all that he or she has to offer. Or when a kick up the pants has more of a chance than a pat on the back. Miklos was a carrot and stick man – he did not let me get away with a single thing. The day after I had been dining with him and his family in a lovely suburb of the Hungarian capital city he would ignore the fact that my heels were giving me pain. 'Get on with it ... get on with it', he would say, and hit me on the back of the head. He's a big guy. Then he'd say: 'You can win. You can win. I know you can win'. Or 'Tessa, you are good. You know you are the best'. It was an American-style 'psych'-up. He had a lot of confidence in me. The truth was he had more confidence in me than I had in myself.

Rumours in England suggested that I went out to Hungary to be put on anabolic steroids. Perhaps it was logical to think so because there is no doubt that they are used extensively in Communist countries and in Britain, too, but that is a later story. Miklos told me that at the Bislett Games in Oslo a British official had gone up to him and said 'I hear you're helping Tessa now'. He replied that I was very fit and confident, to which came the response: 'I hope you're not going to pump all those anabolic steroids into her'. Miklos was very angry. He told me to be very careful of that person. There was vindictiveness and envy in the remark. I told him I wasn't surprised – there is always someone who wants to undermine you.

On the fourth visit to Hungary I went over to receive what in motoring terms would be the final trim. Wilf and Miklos knew I was ready, and that belief from an outstanding coach and a javelin-thrower whom Wilf considered the best of all time, was confidence indeed. It would be entirely my temperament on test, not my condition.

My other spring trip was to Lanzarote, the camp provided by the International Athletes' Club for pre-Olympic warm-weather train-ing. I was delayed for a few days before flying to the Canary Isles because of my sister's wedding, but when eventually I joined Wilf's gang it was to take part in an excellent documentary by Yorkshire Television, which included me in a revealing light blue bikini.

Wilf hurried around trying to fix an early foreign competition for me. It was all too typical that when I rang the Board to see whether there was anything handy I was informed that Fatima had taken up a particular option. With Andy Norman as her confidant and her mother, Margaret, the national coach, it was not particularly surprising. So Wilf persuaded officials to allow me to throw alongside the men at a Carnegie College meeting that included firemen and policemen. As one of the competitors threw over 70 metres, I had a target and was pleased enough with 66.14 metres.

Four days later, with Miklos a special spectator, I had no trouble at all in reaching 68.58 metres at Bolzano in Italy. I knew I was on course and confirmed it at the Crystal Palace Olympic trials on 6 June with 67.02 metres. Ladbrokes, the bookmakers, had me at 14–1 for the Olympic title, Fatima at 2–1. I wish I had been a betting woman! I could have retired. After winning at an international meeting in Florence, I headed for Antrim to throw at Mary Peters' track meeting, hoping that there would be strong opposition, preferably including Fatima and one or two other Olympic contenders. Fatima did not turn up but Trina Solberg was there and I managed to beat her with 68.88 metres. Then on to windy Birmingham for a rather pointless international match before I finally caught up with the elusive Miss Whitbread in the Peugeot-Talbot Games at Crystal Palace. We had a see-sawing, highly-exciting match which she won by eight centimetres to my 67.88 metres. It was what we both needed at that point and although I was fouled out with a 68 to 69 metres there was no need to complain. I was feeling better and better.

At least I was until I let myself be persuaded by the ubiquitous and powerful Andy Norman to return to windy Birmingham for a second throw-out with Fatima. I discovered two things in the Alexander Stadium; that Fatima had a greater reservoir of stamina and that I was still terrified of rain-soaked runways. Miklos was there with my boyfriend, Clement Procope, and apparently he kept muttering 'Jab in, jab in, your left leg!'. No chance of that, I was running – or rather walking – scared and I was creeping in and nursing my left leg. It may have been a stupid thing to do and, of course, Fatima sank me by more than 4 metres. I went up to her and said: 'Well done, Fats'. She replied 'If you think 67 is a good throw, then you don't know what a good throw is'. That was enough for me. Diplomatic relations were more or less broken off.

Wilf, believe it or not, was pleased. He was delighted that I was the underdog because he thought he knew just how much I could bite when I was cornered. He called it 'psychological fodder' and I am interested in the fact that Seb Coe was subjected to a similar bitter harvest of words from the press before flying to the States for six weeks of pre-Olympic training. Nevertheless, I needed a final test-bed before going to California and Potsdam in East Germany looked as good a place as any for there, in the meeting on 21 July, Petra Felke and Antje Kempe would be out to prove that their absence from the Olympic Games would devalue that competition. Another deed, another day, said I and went out their with nothing more in mind that a sound throw. It came with a 69.72 metres while

Felke excelled herself with 74.24 to Kempe's 71.56. They both looked very sharp, blonde Felke, even smaller than me, using the new Sunbeat Diana javelin that I was finding so aerodynamic. I was consistent, bold and my leg was now coming through crisply, just as I wanted. I could not help but be impressed by Felke. Somehow I knew she would win on that day but I was really grateful that I had gone to Potsdam because it cleared my mind of the foolish doubts about technique that had beset me since the Birmingham fiasco. Miklos walked over to me and said: 'You're ready'. No more.

I had no time after that to go home to see my parents but I had to see Dr Durie, for a minor crisis had overcome me. I returned on the Sunday flight out to Los Angeles two days later. I could not stop shaking. My legs were out of control and my mind a wreck: the time was near. Nervous apoplexy had struck. Dr Durie talked to me long and sensibly, checked my Achilles' tendons and told me I was in fine condition. He wouldn't have told me if I hadn't been. Then came another of those routines that sound ridiculous in the cold light of tomorrow but today are the most comforting, I-am-ready-to-beat-the-world motivations possible. It went like this: 'You are the best in the world. You are the best technically. You have Wilf. You have Miklos and you've got me'. Whenever I threw, I was to think: 'Soar like an eagle, soar, soar'. I believed. I took it seriously. Looking back, I smile but it was vitally important then because I needed the confidence. I wanted to soar and I was not always sure how I should take off.

I rang home from Heathrow. My parents said: 'We know you will do your best'. My brothers were more aggressive: 'Go get 'em, Tess'.

CHAPTER SEVEN

Good Buddies

Marea Hartman encourages in her athletes – she likes to call them 'my gels' – the attitude of pupil to headmistress, which in a way I suppose she is. There is absolutely nothing wrong with this for she has responsibility to a lot of parents for safeguarding their girls from at least some of the many temptations that may pass their way. Good order, too, is not assisted by the absence of the rule of law. So far, there have been no arguments. Contrary to what you may have read in lurid Sunday papers, the vast majority of athletics takes place far away from bed, although there are one or two exceptions. It is no secret that Marea likes a gin or two or that on one occasion she was accompanied on a foreign trip by a male companion. In general, however, she has stuck firmly to her standards.

When she refused to let five well-known athletes into the TSB WAAA championships just before the Games, she was justified according to the rule book, even if the sponsors might have raised a quizzical eyebrow. I think she was silly to do this and her attitude showed little regard for the enhancement of our chances in Los Angeles, surely of prime concern to her association. Neither did it take account of the wishes of the spectators who bothered to turn up – in the event there were more ladies named on the meeting programme than there were in the Crystal Palace seats. I badly needed pre-Olympic competition and this was practically my last chance. 'My dear,' she replied, 'the entries were late and you didn't have your cheque in for £2.50.' It is her proudest boast that all her 'gels' pay out of their own pockets and also finance their own board and lodging, for some of them a considerable expenditure. When the meeting moved to Birmingham last year, there had been some relaxation of her unbending dictatorship. Yet in her own way, I think she believed she was playing it fair by all the girls. Her next move was anything but fair: in fact, an utter breach of all she alleged she stood for.

You could just as easily imagine Margaret Thatcher writing for the *Yorkshire Miner* as you could Marea appearing in the *News of the World*. Imagine the athletics world's amazement, then, when her revelations, written in crispest Hartman style, were spread across two pages of that paper. I was at training camp in Point Loma, San Diego, when I discovered I was the star of the piece having, she related, been caught in my bra and pants by a surprised monk. There was more of that type of insulting innuendo, including the suggestion that I was always running around in the nude. Frankly, my first reaction was to sue her. Zola Budd and Shirley Strong were also badly stung and we all felt that we had been badly let down. We had always regarded her as a motherly figure, stern and starchy sometimes, prone to exaggeration but usually helpful towards us all. We cared about her and this was her response: now we felt insecure when she was in our company. I cannot for the life of me understand why she wrote such things, above all because as WAAA secretary and, let me be fair, a dutiful team manager, she was in a position of trust. Not only that, she got her facts wrong. The incident she referred to occurred in a nunnery in Dublin on the one occasion I out-threw Ruth Fuchs. We were playing the fool and Shirley Thomas locked me out of our room when along came a somewhat shocked nun. Not as good a story, but the true version. I have since received an apology from Marea. I think she was appalled at what she had done. I don't know how much she was paid.

Team management can be a very ticklish business, particularly when officials find that among their number is one who prefers to live it up rather more ostentatiously than he or she should. Such a man was the elderly doctor who accompanied the England team during a 1983 international in Eastern Europe. For most of the time, this good doctor was in his cups, consuming quantities of brandy until he was nearly senseless. On a day out riding in the hills, he wandered round asking anyone within distance where he could find a brandy. Verona Elder and a couple of girls were so nervous about him they would not ask for some pills they wanted because they were frightened he would give them the wrong thing. We complained to Marea as head of delegation but it was hard to see what she could do. I must add here that our usual doctors, David Archibald and Andrew Matthews, are sympathetic and first-class. I don't think their colleague has been invited back.

At least Marea leavens her strictness with a sense of fun – at one banquet we even went on stage and played the drums together. Another official, Margaret Oakley, would be more suitable as abbess of a convent. In Prague once, I went to collect a pair of shorts that had been sent to us by Adidas. You will have to wait, was her attitude. It was as though she had paid for the kit out of her own pocket, and was saying 'stand at the back of the room and wait. I'll see if you deserve them'.

The WAAA structure is archaic, with Marea presiding magisterially, filling in little black books for expenses, deciding, for instance, that we should not wear certain shorts and shirts because they are too revealing – what she thought of Strongy's leotard, I shiver to think. I had problems with the bigger T-shirts because the javelin chafed the material against my shoulder, yet I found it almost impossible to make a case that would be acceptable to them for a smaller one. But these fixed laws did not extend to officials. When I went to receive the Lillian Board trophy, there was Vera Sells, a WAAA representative, blowing clouds of smoke across the platform. How, I wonder, would Marea have reacted if I had accepted the award with a cigarette dangling from my lips? Thank goodness men such as Andy Norman and Frank Dick are tugging the WAAA in the wake of the newer, professionally-run men's side. I like Marea. But I don't like one law for us and one law for them.

I had to dig my heels in over the flight to California. Arrangements had been made for me to leave three days after Wilf, who was travelling with Peter Elliott, and four or five after Fatima. It is necessary to acclimatise for as long as possible and it also seemed impractical to be away from my coach at such a critical time when we were working hard on putting an edge to my speed. So I was awkward about it, demanding the same rights as Fatima, a stance that eventually paid off. I went out on the same 'plane as my rival to be followed a few hours later by Wilf and Andy Norman. We waited for them and we all climbed aboard the bus for a two-hour journey. Well, almost all. Andy, Fatima and her mother took a hire car to a first-class hotel. There was no doubt in my mind now whose team Andy was on.

It didn't really matter. I shared a room with my chum, Vanessa Head, just as I had in Helsinki. She is a gentle Welsh giant, dark-haired and entirely feminine, perhaps too much so for she lacks 'animal' in her discus-throwing. Our headquarters was the Nazarine College, Point Loma, a religious institution that had its own athletics facilities. To put it kindly, because I think in principle the idea of a week or so away from the pressures of the Los Angeles athletes' village was sound, the facilities were variable, some rather more befitting a penal institution. Daley arrived five days before we moved north and I have to say that I have seen him fitter. He had been the victim of an accident shortly before; a vaulting pole had snapped and slashed him across the back. He admitted that he was not as fit as he had been and on the night before his competition I visited his room where he was sniffing constantly. I asked the brash and beautiful Daley what was wrong with him. He said he always sniffed when he was very nervous. So much for the image of the impervious, imperious D.T. I said 'Get in there'. He did. What a man! His advice on facing the big day was highly constructive and, training together on the javelin, I think I helped him because at a crucial time in his decathlon, he knew that he could come back at Jurgen Hingsen he had improved so much.

I didn't help him half as much as he helped me, though. I had been warming up in a relaxed sort of way and one throw landed rather nearer to the 80-metres mark than should be allowed out of competition. The javelin just seemed to float on and on towards Mexico and prompted me to challenge Daley to an informal contest. I took a longer approach run and there was a drop in performance of about 10 metres. Daley noticed this, too, and gave vigorous support to Wilf's argument that my run-up should be shortened and more explosive. It was no coincidence that back home Brian

Newman had been trying to make me see the same point. I decided to follow their advice.

The British team is famous for togetherness, and nearly infamous for our tricks. The boys know I am game for a laugh and they regularly set me up, particularly Wilbert Greaves and his clique. One lunchtime after finishing a hard stint with Daley, Wilf said that I should have lunch and idle around for the rest of the day because I had earned a rest. Our third javelin girl, Sharon Gibson, and I had just played a round of cards with Zola Budd when Sharon went outside. I shouted to her but, as she appeared not to have heard me, I walked to the door and stood smiling. That was when Wilbert turned the hosepipe on me – with the television cameras rolling.

Perhaps the most unfortunate thing about Point Loma was that the distance away from the Memorial Coloseum practically ruled out many of us attending the opening ceremony. When we arrived at the camp we were told that journey and accreditation time to Los Angeles would be three hours and that we would have to return the same day after many hours standing in the heat, unless we wished to pay for our own accommodation. This in turn would have meant missing nearly two days' training. It would not have hurt the Board to pay a few 40-dollar air fares to ensure a fair athletics contingent among the horse-riders, rifle-shooters and gymnasts. A few of the more independent spirits broke the rules and went anyway while David Ottley decided it was such an historic occasion that he would stay in the Olympic village at UCLA to be able to march around the track behind the British flag. Later he was to see the flag rising just for him.

The British team management was superb, the best I have encountered. Lyn Davies served as men's manager and my dearest friend, Mary Peters, kept order among the girls, ably helped by another former athlete, Pam Piercy. Mary is an angel, not always of mercy, but certainly of good sense. She remained impartial about the needs of her athletes and never suggested favouritism to me or anyone else – she just isn't the type. But we do have a special rapport and I felt in my heart that she particularly wanted things to go right for me. Maybe that's her secret and every girl felt that way. Two quiet words of correction from her were more effective than a thundering volley from anyone else, for not only did we know that she was 100 per cent on the side of the athletes but also that she had done all we had, and more, herself.

I know she believed in me as a heptathlete because she was not in the least surprised by my 1981 successes. I remember watching television, rapt, as she went through her gold medal sequence in the 1972 Olympic Games in Munich. That smile, as wide and warm as the equator, when she landed, stretched out after clearing the high-jump bar; the sheer joy – I hope I gave that feeling to people. Then came the 200 metres, her legs pitter-pattering down the track and finally crossing the line to a reception that surpassed all others. A year later I competed against her at Warley and, do you know, I don't recall her at all. What a dizzy little baggage I must have been! Or should I excuse myself by saying that I concentrated so hard I don't remember a thing? Even then, I wanted to be like her and I still do. She could have left Northern Ireland without anyone accusing her of desertion. It was typical of her that she preferred to stay, a Liverpool girl whom the province had adopted, despite numerous threats and the untimely death of her coach, Buster McShane. The one subject on which we differ is religion. With her purity and calm acceptance of life, it would seem to me that she has a religious vocation. But, no, as I said earlier, she doesn't believe in God. She lives for each day. Sometimes it must be the only way to exist and keep your sanity in Northern Ireland.

The sadness for athletics was that Lyn, Mary and Pam all retired after Los Angeles, each of them disturbed by trends away from the style of management to which they were accustomed and into tennis-like individualism where people go into the sport only for what they can get out of it. The worst of Mary's forebodings appear to be coming true.

Fatima missed out on Point Loma, a decision that was absolutely hers to make but one that rather suited Sharon Gibson and I because we consequently had more track time. Among the crowd there was a lost little soul who was due to face a test probably unparalleled in Olympic history. Zola Budd had been introduced to

Britain as a marketable commodity, a piece of breath-taking opportunism by the Government, the British Board and the *Daily Mail* that made a curio out of the then 18-year-old girl who wanted only to run. She was rich pickings that year and I didn't like the idea. I have less than no time for the South African regime and although I am greatly opposed to boycotts, the one aimed at apartheid has become justifiable by results. Furthermore, Zola's inclusion cost a British girl her 3000 metres place – if, as was possible at one stage, that girl had been Wendy Sly, a silver medal would have been sacrificed on the altar of expediency. But sitting across the room, twiddling with a pack of cards, was not a political cipher but a young and lonely fellow athlete. I asked if she would like to play cards with Sharon and I and when she replied that she didn't know how, we settled down to teach her. From then on Zola belonged and whenever she went wrong, I said 'Get out of here, Budd, stop bloody cheating'. She had a room of her own, quite rightly because privacy was important to her at this stage, and, anyway, it forced her out to socialise. She's a smashing girl, but was then still very much a child out in the wide world. My competition was before hers and so I gave her a goodbye hug the evening before I set off for the village which was our staging post for the Games themselves. Sharon dropped into my room later on and handed me a present. This was not Sharon's style and I thought either she wants money or a drink out of me or it's another damned practical joke. I accused her of joking. Hadn't she once locked me out of our room and got on with a pillow fight while I was hammering away, not even dressed, at the door? No, she said, it's genuine, from Zola. Inside was a fluffy dog, a little beggar dog, with the most beautiful message: 'Thank you for being my friend'. I admit I was choked with emotion. Obviously we had all been struck by how lonely she was, now she was really reaching out to someone. This wasn't politics: she was flesh and blood. Once settled into my village quarters, I decided to respond. I bought a toy chihuaha dog, black and white with a pink tongue hanging out and sent it to her, enclosing a card wishing her luck with her race. I wanted to remind her that in the British team we are all one but, honestly, it did not strike me until a long time afterwards that the dog was black and white. I wasn't trying to be symbolic, just a friend. A couple of days after my victory – and I had kept her present with me as a talisman – she wrote to me saying that she did not know how to express herself to an Olympic champion and congratulated me in such a touching way that when I saw her before her semi-final I felt real affection for her. We just hugged again. In her spectacles she looks very serious, student-ish, and is, indeed, intelligent. She is also warm and giving and still very inexperienced. The day before her ill-fated final I asked her how everything was going. She replied, very softly, that she needed to go a bit faster and that Marcica Puica, the eventual gold medallist, had dug her in the ribs. I told her she had to fight; that this was the Olympic Games and that some runners could be bitches. Then I suggested that the next day she should wear spikes. It was as though I knew something was going to happen and I felt guilty about that. I waited with Mary Peters as Zola left the Coloseum in tears. We were sad, for being booed after the Decker collision must have been a shocking experience. I was approached by an American radio reporter who asked for a comment from a competitor who came from the black part of England. I let fly at that: what did he know about England? Then he claimed Zola had fouled Decker and I launched into Mary Decker for the way she had behaved. I doubt if he used that tape. It now seems that Zola is on her way to becoming a great runner, a great British runner at that. I hope so. Her dignity has ensured the admiration of most people and I think the more recent demonstrations against her have been futile, unnecessary and counter-productive.

David Ottley's silver medal in the javelin preceded my competition and was a great boost for us all. Once under Margaret Whitbread's wing in Essex, he had moved to Telford and for a short time we had trained together. He was unfailing in his support and was one of the few people who forecast that I would finish ahead of Fatima at Los Angeles. David suspected that Mrs Whitbread had not wanted him selected and this did not endear her daughter's cause to him. I watched from the athletes' section of the stands when he qualified but it was so hot and humid on the day of his final, also the eve of my qualifying round, that I decided it would not be sensible to sit outside again for any length of time. I had never seen him so thoroughly in tune mentally and in that mood the reputations of opponents mean nothing. His block-mates, Daley, Donovan Reid, Mike MacFarlane and Brad McStravick, were some of the liveliest guys around and how we roared our approval as we watched his presentation on television. It gave us all heart.

The next day was to be the girls' turn: Fatima, Sharon and me. Fatima had chosen to stay in a hotel and because she had not been through the routine as we had, was involved in a last-minute panic because she forgot her accreditation. Mary Peters dashed to the hotel for it and arrived back just in time for Fatima to compete in the round before me, throwing what turned out to be the best of the day, 65.30 metres.

In the morning Mary had woken me up at seven and I had strolled to Sharon's compartment and hauled her out of bed too for breakfast half an hour later. The memories of Moscow were back with me and although I tried to laugh them off, I was only half-joking when I said I would shave off all my hair if I failed. A Russian did that one year and it seemed a reasonable sacrificial offering to the vengeful Press. Otherwise we were silent. This was it. Max Jones, national throwing events coach, and Mary were down-to-earth and sensible. Mary held our hands for a moment and said to each of us 'You'll do well, kid'. We checked out of the village at half past eight and I fussed over whether I should wear a headband, the kind of meaningless thing I do when I am really nervous.

Moscow had taught me to take things one step at a time. I concentrated entirely on qualification, determined not to freeze. Fatima came through the waiting-room having qualified and wished us good look. I congratulated her on her throw and thought she must be really sharp until I saw the video later on and realised that there had been a tremendous amount of effort in her throw. At last we were out in the stadium, just as the sun burned away the remnants of smog. Technically, I must admit, my first and only throw was terrible: arms right above my head, the final stride so long that I had to pull back, thus sending the javelin searing to the left.

Really it was no more than a toss but it went 61.58 metres and I was in the final. Even so, I wanted to go through on a note of confidence so I asked Sharon whether I should take another. She replied firmly that I should save it and to this day I am grateful because I remained intensely hungry for another one, a special 'biggie'. Sharon did marvellously, qualifying with a personal best of 60.88 metres so that Britain filled three of the dozen places. Tiina was there, too.

At last I had said my final farewell to my Moscow hangover. I did not stop smiling the whole day. Then came the realisation that ahead of me was the greatest day of my life for, win or lose, I was ready to show the world what I was made of.

CHAPTER EIGHT

Olympic Gold

I wish each of us was given the choice of a day we could keep in a bottle, complete, to be opened whenever we wished; to be able to re-live a day with its colours, smells, emotions, conversations, incidents, small problems perhaps and, being human, the most significant moments. The day in my case would be 6 August, 1984. As another hot, choking afternoon turned into the clear, deep blue of a Californian evening, I won the Olympic gold medal for the women's javelin and uncorked the dreams of a dozen and more years. But back to the bottled essence of 6 August that would remind me of much I had missed during the preliminaries which passed, apparently as unremarkable as any others, before the competition. I am sure they did not. I think all the signs pointed to my victory and I should like to examine each one, from every angle, like some professor at an archeological dig. From real life I recall that Sharon and I fiddled the day away, me worrying about that silly black headband and whether it mattered that I looked my best. Mary was around, smiling generously, and Max Jones, with his sly humour and good sense, was constantly in the background. Vanessa went off to do a training session, having composed a note, with Helen Barnett, that said: 'Good luck, kids. This is your day'. I had a rubdown, laid out my kit, decided to wear the headband, then not. Then we were high on our adrenalin, rather like children before they go on holiday. On reflection, it may be just as well there are no memory bottles. I couldn't live through such fear again. In my nervousness I stumbled against a shelf in my room, knocking down a card from Barbara Richards. It read: 'Happy are those who dream dreams and are ready to pay the price to make them come true'. I smiled inside and I knew I was ready.

Eventually, we were aboard the bus which was to take about 40 minutes to travel from the elegant Los Angeles suburb of Westwood, along roads of Spanish-style homes, into the drab, industrial belt around the Memorial Coloseum. My fidgets turned to inner panic when I realised that the bus was taking much longer than it should to inch its way through the barriers of rush-hour traffic. Would we be the first athletes disqualified because of lateness, irretrievably stuck somewhere in the metal jungle of Los Angeles while ten other girls played out the Olympic story? Suddenly two police outriders appeared, dressed in all that sinister space-age kit, to lead us from the front, hooters blaring right to the stadium in time for the warm-up. I went straight to the area we called 'the pits' and started technique work with Wilf.

My coach, small, dark and moustachioed, had taken on a new identity. For the duration of the Olympic Games he had become one Matias Prats, a Spanish television commentator who, peculiarly, spoke only West Country English. It is fair to say that Wilf had fallen foul of authority, in the form of his ex-employers, the British Athletics Board. He could have no serious quarrel with the fact that he was not part of team arrangements, many coaches were not, but no visible attempts were made to help him either with accommodation or tickets. He is a resourceful chap, however, and armed with a sack of cents he began ringing contacts, alighting on Russ Hodge, a well-known athlete who was also a member of a born-again Christian group, the Church of Grace. The church made arrangements for him to stay at the home of John Disderdick, a millionaire living in the hills at Studio City, who was also kind enough to house in magnificent style two other coaches in the same predicament. Sometimes American generosity is breathtaking. They even transported Wilf night and day to the Coloseum. While the Board paid for his stay at Point Loma and organised entry to the warm-up areas, they would not provide privileged tickets on the days his four athletes competed. Determined as ever, Wilf settled down at the media accreditation office for as long as it took a lady official who admired his gall to come up with a pass. When Señor Matias Prats telexed that he wasn't going to be commentating for Spanish television, Wilf was in there like a shot and, accreditation card draped around his neck, he was free to sit among the mystified Spaniards in their section of the stadium press box. So Wilf was able to watch from a prime position after pre-competition preparation with his athletes.

So here he was, talking confidently, boosting me up in 'the pits' when Fatima walked in looking decidedly less flustered than she had before the preliminary round. I had started to throw in the second warm-up section when Tiina Lillak arrived, walking without a limp although there were reports that she had ankle problems. I don't doubt that they were true, as the evidence later proved, but Tiina would be the last person to put forward an excuse. She knew I had been suffering for four years, and what was she supposed to do – let me win? I warmed up for 15 minutes, doing strides and little arm-jabs while nearby Sharon was being briefed by John Moogan, my former coach, and Fatima by Mrs Whitbread. Then I tried a few long throws and I knew for certain that I was in superb shape, confident, composed, ready for the battle of my life. At call-time, Wilf shook my hand a bit to make it feel loose, gave me the usual peck on the cheek and left to become Matias Prats again. I felt as lonely as I am ever likely to. I beckoned Sharon to come on and Fatima joined us as we walked, with a show of nonchalance none of us could have felt, to a bus for the final countdown: it was more like Gary Gilmore's final minutes before being shot than I cared to think about. So on to the pre-competition warm-up area where I went through a hard routine of throws, one of them with a ball which stuck high in a net. I was about to try to retrieve it when Mary hurried along. 'For God's sake don't jump and rupture your legs again', she said, spotting a concrete slab that would have ended my hopes there and then had I landed badly. Just as I shook the ball free, the red light showed and we were on our way. Max and Lyn wished us well, Mary gave us a hug and a kiss and we walked into the stadium, feeling, (at least I was) as though we were a team of three against the world. That will never happen again, I am sure; Fatima and I have such different temperaments and are no longer more than reluctant colleagues. On this one occasion, however, the first time three British throwers had ever reached an Olympic final, we had the comfort of one another's presence.

Our spikes were checked and then we had to wait an interminable five minutes while the women's marathon runners came through. Walking down the tunnel was the longest journey of my life; down where the light was at a pinpoint an insistent, intimidating roar almost physically warned us off. We had to urge ourselves towards the glowing, bluish light of evening, and once through the tunnel and into the dense air I could hear Sue Morley's husband Colin shouting: 'Go get 'em, Tess!'. Close to the entrance, I sat down and put on my shoes, ready at last and oblivious to one of the Games' major dramas, Gabriela Andersen-Scheiss, subconscious, tottering her last lap of pain, courage and madness in the first women's marathon of Olympic history. I have to say that for us, her heroism was another delay and I sensed that Tiina was as impatient as I was that what we regarded as a minor contest between outrageously tired ladies should impinge on the real stuff of battle. Would we ever start? Then when we marched down the back straight in crocodile fashion, against the echoing din in which discernible voices cried 'Come on Fatima!' 'Come on Tessa!'. Beside the runway we were free to rush for javelins. Lillak, her Finnish team-mate Tuula Laaksalo and I chose Sandvik Dianas, Fatima the Apollo. I asked an official to hold my tape for me and measured my run-up, which we had reduced by 30 feet to 73 feet only a week or so before. Sharon borrowed the tape, we were allowed two practice throws and I felt perfect – entirely self-composed.

Fatima threw before me, just as she had on the last two occasions she had beaten me. There was no chance that I was going to flop in this one though, even if she had produced another Helsinki-style flier. I knew that if my technique was right, if I banged in my shoulder at the end of a well-controlled run, the javelin would go a long way – it was vital that I did this because there are almost no exceptions to the rule that a false start on the first will be followed by a worse second. And that is a third of your six trials. Fatima threw compactly to 64.52 metres and I knew I could beat that. I had become so preoccupied that Sharon had to tap me on the shoulder and remind me: 'Come on, it's your turn'.

After stripping down, my last thought before the run-up was 'please God, make it right', and I was on my way. Everything seemed still – I was going to give 100 per cent. Onwards, onwards ... I told myself: 'Come on, Tessa, get it right now, just hit hard. Please God, let it be right this time'. My leg was straight, my body square, I followed my throw right out and finished with a metre or so to spare of the disqualification line. I knew it was long. But how long? With one bounce it landed on the 70-metre mark and I kept repeating to myself: 'Make it near 70 and everyone will have to fight'. Wilf had reckoned 68.50 metres would win the gold medal in these still conditions in which you had to throw high and accurately to float the javelin on what breeze there was. I was half-way through my walk towards my tracksuit before the electronic scoreboard registered 69.56 metres and I realised with the inner certainty of a poker player who believes he has the winning hand that ... no, I could not afford thoughts like those. 'Just relax, stay cool ...'. Tiina went in with 61.14 metres and looked very worried.

We reached the crux of the competition in the second round. Fatima improved to 65.42 metres but failed to catch me while I made 66.56 which gave me the confidence to believe there was another very big throw in me, if needed. Then it was Tiina's turn. I could see she was gathering everything together for a knock-out throw; the signs were all there. Two or three times she went into short, practice routines. Then she was into her run, fast, determined as a raging bull. She is tall-ish, fair and sinewy and has excellent technique. But this was more, this was her last throw and as she thrust that leg down, it was almost as if she had declared 'this is win or bust'. I felt myself tingling and waited for the board to illuminate us. It showed 69.00 metres and I was as certain as humanly possible that she would not better my first throw. We had shattered the field and Tiina had shattered herself. Indeed, it now became obvious that she was in serious trouble with her ankle. When they called for her third round throw, she failed to respond. I went up to her and said: 'It's your turn, Tiina'. She replied: 'I can't take any more'. I admit my sympathy was diluted by relief for she was, after all, world champion and my chief rival.

The other rounds brought shuffles among the lesser places with Fatima being pursued by Laaksalo who produced 66.40 metres to overtake her in the fourth round. I could not criticise Fatima's fighting instincts because she answered with 67.14 in the fifth, reaching into the depths of her resilient nature. After the fourth round, I let my mind wander a bit, thinking sentimental stuff such as 'This is for my Mum and everyone who is watching at home'. And I even remembered the lady in Walsall who predicted before Moscow that I would be all right next time. In the circumstances my 66.86 metres in the fifth trial was very reasonable and then, as the realisation of my achievement grew, I found my whole body was going cold as I waited for the sixth and last throw: part of me wanted to stop then but I felt I had a duty to complete all the throws. It was only then that I felt it would be right to respond to the cheers that echoed around tier after tier of the now-floodlit stadium.

I was Olympic champion from the moment Fatima failed to register with her last attempt. Me! Olympic champion, Olympic record-breaker, first British girl to win a throwing event, fourth since the war to win an athletics gold, first black girl to win a throwing gold. And I was in heaven. I fell to my knees and made a two-armed gesture of triumph. A spectator leapt the fence, kissed me, said 'Tessa, you're a darling', and draped the Union flag around my shoulders. Fatima and I embraced but unfortunately Sharon had failed to qualify for the final three throws and couldn't be there. Tiina, too, had left, propped between two medical attendants, her injured foot held above the ground. Fatima suggested that we should do a lap of honour and, as a winning team, we did although not without a small controversy. At the top end of the stadium, an official jumped out and halted us by holding out his arm and then grasping mine. 'Would you mind stopping, Ma'am?' he said, 'Carl Lewis is about to jump.' I was infuriated. 'How dare you touch me! Who do you think Carl Lewis is? I've just won a gold medal and he didn't stop for me to throw.' He let us through, muttering apologies.

We waited in line for the medal ceremony. Suddenly as the opening fanfare began I was frighteningly nervous again. There was a shout: 'Women's javelin. Victory protocol. Presentation of the women's javelin'. I had to try to walk with good posture, which presented rather a problem because my knees were weak and my poor heart was racing. Behind the number one place on the podium, my head was buzzing and I was so feeble that I could not at first climb to the top. I was told at the presentation that I had done myself and my country proud, a sentiment that set off the first trickle of tears. The crowd roared in acclamation and I was alone again, with fulfilled dreams and momentary thoughts of how I came to be in this place, in the only place for an athlete to be. Then Tiina hobbled beside me and Fatima after her. The band played 'God Save The Queen' and 97,000 spectators, plus multi-millions more watching on television, looked on as tears streamed down my face and into a wider grin than Lenny Henry's. Whatever else happens in my life, this was the greatest moment, the time I felt immortal. Barbara Richards had written to me at the worst of times 'happy are those who dare to dream dreams'. How much I owed to good people like her. I closed my eyes and thought 'Thank God, it's all over'. And from the bottom of my heart, I don't think I have ever meant anything so much. Tiina, Fatima and I hugged and the electronic scoreboard recorded the history:

1 172 Sanderson, Tessa GBR 69.56
2   97 Lillak, Tiina FIN 69.00
3 181 Whitbread, Fatima GBR 67.14
4   95 Laaksalo, Tuula FIN 66.40
5 288 Solberg, Trine NOR 64.52
6 140 Thyssen, Ingrid FRG 63.26
7 131 Peters, Beate FRG 62.34
8 395 Smith, Karin USA 62.06

Within minutes, I was whisked towards the BBC cameras and my old friends David Coleman, Ron Pickering and Stuart Storey. I was standing with Fatima when the director came over and said he was ready. Fatima shouted for her mother to come along but I intervened and said that if they didn't mind I should like Wilf to be with me. Perhaps that was selfish, yet I do not think I have anything to apologise for. Fatima and I had shared the plaudits carrying the flag on our lap of honour; it seemed only right that my coach should be with me during the first interview. Not that he said much if anything. Wilf chatters a lot but on this occasion he was utterly speechless – he couldn't find a word to say. I was not much better, the only thing that seemed to make much sense was my thanks to everyone in Yorkshire, Leeds and Telvista. Tongue-tied, 'The eagle has landed'. It had indeed.

There were two ceremonies left. One involved a woman in a white coat who had taken to following me and the entourage who had helped so much over the previous few weeks: Mary, Pam, Dr Archibald and several others. Miss White Coat said: 'Miss Sanderson, you must come now', and dogged my footsteps as I made for Frank Dick, who had never permitted his bad relationship with Wilf to interfere with his duties towards me. Indeed, I found him immensely considerate and felt that he, sitting beside the track, deserved another of the hugs I had been dispensing so liberally. Why not? I was really bubbling. And I always felt that Frank for some reason especially wanted me to win. The lady still wouldn't go away, so I reversed the process and this time followed her to the drug-testing area where I had to give a sample. Weeing into a little bottle when you have just won an Olympic gold medal is akin to threading that camel through the eye of a needle, especially when a lady in a white coat keeps staring at you. It took half an hour, three hours less, at least, than it took Kathy Cook when she won her 400 metres bronze. The other duty was to meet the Press, many of whom had written off my chances long before we arrived in Los Angeles. I resisted taunting them. They are, as they constantly remind competitors, only doing their jobs. Zola's dog looked down on them from the table which held the microphones.

I rang home then. My brother Eric answered. All he did was laugh and say 'Well done. You did it, Tess'. Eventually he told me my father had missed seeing my victory. Apparently, when he got back from having a pint at his local, The Castle, he went to bed with the comment: 'Wake me up when Tessa's won'. To his eternal embarrassment, they did. It was about five o'clock in the morning in Britain but it sounded as though there was a party going already. Dad called me his 'darling, golden girl' and Mum quietly told me how wonderfully I had done.

It was late when I returned to the village and I rushed up to my room expecting the whole gang to be there. Instead, they had decked the place out with balloons and hung the traditional flag on my door, too. There were messages – from Marea Hartman: 'Tessa Wins Gold Medal Naked' (I realised that was a joke); and from Margaret Whitbread: 'Now you are truly the greatest javelin-thrower Britain has ever had'. I thought, that's nice. I really was so dizzy with my triumph that I failed to spot the sarcasm. In fact, after her 'well done' beside the podium, Margaret Whitbread has never uttered further words in my direction, although she may have communicated in other ways.

The girls had waited for so long for me to turn up that they thought I had gone on elsewhere, so I flopped into bed, slept fitfully and woke up with my Achilles' tendon throbbing wickedly and my legs numb with exhaustion. I went quickly for some massage, then had a champion sleep. In the morning I knew I had become famous because I was on the Terry Wogan show and then, saddest of all for me, I returned Sonia's call. My golden twin from Edmonton was missing for the first time in ages and hers was the voice I most wanted to hear at that moment. Then came the telegrams, four or five dozen of them, including a message from another old friend, Joan Alison, that said starkly: 'What took you so long, you old bag?'. The team enjoyed that. The one from Prince Philip was more formal.

Thames Television wanted to fly me back two days before the Games finished to be guest of honour at a celebration of their winning the five-year contract for British athletics. I refused, not only because I wished to watch Seb, Daley and the others or because I wanted to be there at the closing ceremony – although of course, I did – but because I did not feel there was much to celebrate about the BBC losing the contract. Ron Pickering, David Coleman, Stuart Storey and the others were not only top-class commentators and knowledgeable men but also friends whom we had grown to trust and rely on. The BBC's coverage of athletics was expert and as yet ITV have not shown they can do better. Maybe they will, I am not prejudiced about it, but it took years of experience for the BBC to reach the standard they did and it seemed a waste to me that they should be dismissed for what in the long run may prove to be the wrong reason – cash. Athletics, like any other sport, needs expertise and good salesmanship. It doesn't need hype, over-sensationalism or to be used as a 'filler'.

So, after days of celebration, congratulation and saying my thank yous, I was at the most thrilling closing ceremony I have ever been part of. The Americans know how to do this sort of thing, informally and yet with just sufficient dignity and sense of occasion to get by, at least they have in the latter part of the 20th century. How we danced! We waited two hours, itching to get out there into the stadium full of light and excitement and music, Seb carrying the flag and me linking arms with Daley who was not going to miss the chance to display several of his famous T-shirts. The cameras were on us when suddenly he moved me aside to disclose the message spread across his chest: 'Thank you America for a wonderful Games'. It was a beautiful gesture although for a minute I thought he was about to display another one about the second-best athlete in the world being gay.

Underneath the wisecracker is a lovely man trying to get out. Daley was branded a bigmouth after his Olympic gold medal Press conference in which he referred to his conversation with Princess Anne, but anyone who knows him will tell you that it was just his way of having fun, of spoofing away his own nervousness. Cynical? Perhaps he is. But is anyone more cynical than our Press men?

Seb, Daley and I were arm-in-arm wondering whether we could find someone to take a picture of us when someone came up to ask me if I had seen Edwin Moses as he was walking around asking people if they had seen me. I hadn't seen Edwin for three or four years and in the meantime he had married. I think the world of that solemn, sincere man and so I went hunting him out through singing teams and officials who were not keen for me to pass. Finally, I recognised him from the back and moved up to tap him on the shoulder. His great big eyes popped open and he swept me up into his arms with an Olympic-sized hug. He told me about his wife, about how his mother was coping with the death of his father and why he had experienced a little trouble with his speech at the opening ceremony.

The sweet old flatterer said that the greatest thing that had happened to him during the Games was seeing me win my gold medal. Well, it may sound corny on paper but it wasn't, not the way Edwin said it. Suddenly the sky was alight with fireworks, rainbows of colour overhead. He kissed me on the cheek and, typically, came up with the right words: 'These fireworks, they're all for you, Tessa'. And I felt it was true.

CHAPTER NINE

Royal Meetings

It had been 12 years since a British girl won an Olympic gold and who better than the previous gold medallist, Mary Peters, to go to for advice? She was very clear in what she said: 'Look, love, just enjoy yourself. You may never get another chance and, don't forget, a lot of these people are doing it for themselves'. How true! It was a time to remember who had helped in those dog days when it seemed I had as much chance of becoming Olympic champion as I had of leaping the moon. That was why I was so upset at having to turn down my first invitation to compete. It came from Miklos who wanted me on show in Budapest four days after my return to England. He had gone to Los Angeles and had been a constant friend and ally, yet I had explained to him before the final that, come what may, Los Angeles was my last date of the year. I have no doubt that I could have cashed in at meetings all over Europe and yet that was not the point because there were friends I wished to see, thanks to be made and, besides, I was so tired and on such a high that there was no way I could have done justice to myself or to my sport. Miklos and Andy were very pressing and professed not to understand my view, having more or less taken it for granted that I would tour. But I would not bend and I believe that Miklos at least began to appreciate my position. Later I could and would make up for his obvious disappointment.

So I went home to my house in Shadwell Walk, Leeds, driving a Porsche that Hertz had lent me and feeling quite the star. No sooner had I parked than people appeared from everywhere and someone started the street party by playing 'Young, Gifted And Black' – it must have been Clement, he loves that song. The city made a great big fuss of me – the *Yorkshire Post* hosted a huge reception where I even had a chance to chat with the girls I used to work with at Guardian Royal Exchange. Then I made my way to Wednesfield and another great big bash, centred on Wood End Road and The Castle where they splashed out with champagne. Dad, I think, stuck to pints. I could feel the pride they all had in me which meant so much more than all the blandishments of hangers-on, and there were a few of those. I thought that although I could repay my mother dozens of times over for the five pounds she pinched from Dad's trouser pocket, there is no way that a child could ever repay his or her parents for all that they have really sacrificed.

Then came news that soured some of the delight: Telvista went into liquidation. Barry Whitford, a clever and forceful man, had over-reached himself, so the company closed its plush offices and made its employees redundant. I returned their car and, leaving the office for the last, sad time it occurred to me that here I was, an Olympic gold medallist, with no job and something like £1,000 to my name. Clement and I concluded that we should form our own company, Tessa Promotions, and see if we could rely on our own initiative. We did do this but I must report that any story of untold Sanderson riches are laughably untrue. I am a bit of a worrier about where my next pennies are coming from – and I am still worried. I admit to being a spender when I have money but I have never received enormous payments and, even if I had, the British Board rules on trust funds would have prevented me from getting my hands on much cash.

The initial attraction of being invited to smart functions was wearing thin. I would far, far rather have gone to a school than a cocktail party where there are no kids with a gleam in their eyes who want to laugh with excitement and to touch the gold medal; self-satisfaction was the only gleam at some of those other occasions. Towards the end of the year, however, there is a newish variety of dinner, usually held by journalists who have cast their votes to choose the top sports personality. The athletics writers made me their number one girl and so did the Sports Writers' Association at a glamorous night in London at which I was placed next to Princess Anne. We had a good old natter while Seb, sitting on the other side of her, must have wondered just what we had in common – a lot more than you may think, Seb. There was another gong in 1984, the second most prestigious for me: the MBE which actually was announced seconds into 1985. Recipients are told a good deal earlier than that, in my case ten weeks after winning the gold. In all that time, the only limb I had lifted in earnest was my right arm, conveying champagne to my lips; or so it seemed. No jogging, no weights, not even a morning loosener – I was determined to take Mary's advice and wallow in the achievement. I'm no big drinker, in fact, so I suspected nothing specific when I went to see the doctor about stomach cramps that had affected me spasmodically. He diagnosed 'champagne poisoning'. I had put on eight pounds in weight which, considering I was gorging myself at function after function, was not all that much, and now I was paying for it. The price was even higher when I took my place in *The Krypton Factor*, the ITV game show. The contestants, June Croft, Neil Adams and me – all Olympic medallists – were shown the course beforehand and I must say I was rather contemptuous of the 22 obstacles. A piece of cake, I thought, pondering more anxiously on how I would do in the questions section. So I started the course at a fair clip until I began to feel light-headed. When the water jump came I was in trouble, my legs collapsing from exhaustion. Knee-deep, I was praying for help from the Almighty. I was wheezing now and hanging on in the parachute jump for dear life, images passing through my mind of that Swiss girl staggering like a drunk to the finish of the marathon. Neil had passed me and June was behind when I came to the staked-out net under which we had to crawl. There I was, the super-fit Olympic champion, grovelling through the dirt to cries of 'Come on, Tessa!', while I could only gasp 'I'm coming!'. I finished last, too shattered even to think about what an exhibition I had made of myself. That night I was wheezing so loudly in bed that I turned on the light because I thought someone else was in the room.

In the morning, about nine o'clock, Clement rang to say 'You've done it, Tessa. You've done it!'. My first thought was that my exploits of the day before were in the national newspapers – they were! – but he wouldn't have sounded quite so pleased so I asked what he was talking about. 'The MBE. You've got the MBE', he said, and I grinned as he added 'Her Majesty commands you!'. No two ways about that. It was really difficult to follow the instructions to keep the award secret, in particular from my mother to whom I tell everything. I decided the only way I could stop blurting it out was to forget it, just file it away in the back of my mind. I was so successful that it led to another incident, this time with a radio reporter who appeared during one of my few training sessions early that winter. He came closer and closer until I said: 'You're not coming to interview *me*, are you?'. He confirmed that he was.

'What have I done now?' I asked, a little irritated because I was fatigued from doing 150-metre spring repetitions.

'I've come to congratulate you. I'm probably the last of many.'

'No, Los Angeles was only six months ago. You do mean the gold medal don't you?'

'No, I don't. You must know what's happening tonight.'

'I don't. It's just another Sunday, isn't it?'

Wilf came over and, out of the hearing of the radio man, I said: 'That guy was talking to me about the strangest thing. What's he on about?'. Wilf grinned and said: 'Tonight. It's 31 January. New Year's Honours'. At last it dawned on me. Theresa Ione Sanderson MBE. But all I said was: 'We'll look in on television. See if it's true'.

That night Clement and I were sitting on my long settee, chatting with friends who had called. On the news was a long sequence about miners and politicians: I wondered if there would be any room for me until, near the end, the newscaster announced the honour with a smile. I raised a glass of champagne that just happened to be in my hand and shouted 'Oh! Yeah!'. That put the crown on a great year.

There must be telepathy at work when I am doing television shows because I was making a fool of myself playing darts against Fatima in *Game For A Laugh* when the Palace was in touch again. I rang Clement one morning and he said a telegram had just arrived from Buckingham Palace asking me to ring urgently. Clement laughed when I suggested that they might want the MBE back, then I became suddenly and deeply suspicious that I was being set up for another laugh. Clement isn't usually the type but I played along, took a London 'phone number from him and duly called it. A Brigadier answered: 'Oh! Miss Sanderson, I'm so glad you called. Her Majesty the Queen and Prince Philip request the pleasure of your joining them for lunch with eight other guests and four people from the Queen's household'. 'Are you joking?' I asked. He assured me that he most certainly was not. So I accepted, still suspecting a trick, but how do you say: 'Sorry, Your Majesty, I can't make it?'. 'We look forward to meeting you', added the Brigadier. I told the crew outside and I could see straight away that this was no joke. I was to be a guest of the Queen.

It was on St Valentine's Day, 14 February, that I was conveyed in my carriage – a Hertz Jaguar driven by my friend Carol dressed in chauffeur's cap and smart black and yellow uniform – feeling ridiculously regal, to the entrance gates of Buckingham Palace. It was as though everyone knew I was coming, which no doubt they did, for, although the Queen was not waiting on the steps with her corgis in the way I had always pictured it in my imagination, when I showed my pass, the guard saluted and grounded his rifle. I liked that. The salute was repeated by two more guards when I entered the building itself, grinning massively. Through the first door a gentleman was waiting with a 'Good afternoon, Miss Sanderson. Welcome to Buckingham Palace'. This treatment, too, was repeated in the next room where I was asked with infinite politeness if I wished to go to the toilet. I didn't but I was keen to see if the washroom was all marble so I went. Disappointingly, it was like many another.

Finally then, I was flunkeyed to the big morning room, a nervously exhilarated black girl among all that majesty. I must have been the last in because I was introduced to a semi-circle of guests who were waiting for the Queen to arrive. Ten minutes later she came downstairs, wearing a lovely blue crepe-type dress and followed, sure enough, by three corgis. The Duke of Edinburgh completed the train. The Queen, whose wrist was bandaged, was petite and incredibly healthy-looking. She said hello to me and then moved around the semi-circle being introduced. This took a little while and then she returned for a chat that must have lasted 20 minutes. We talked about javelin-throwing and the exercises required, touched on the use of anabolic steroids and discussed Princess Anne's attendance at the Games. 'Did she enjoy them?' I asked. 'Immensely', said the Queen. And then with a trace of a smile: 'She has often told me things about you, especially that occasion when you met at the Variety function. She's a big fan of yours'. I thought 'Heavens, what has she said?' and it was comforting to know that Princess Anne came home for a chinwag with her mum just like I do when something interesting has happened to me. Eventually the Queen said: 'I think we had better go in to lunch, don't you?'. Then came my *faux pas*. 'Yes, I think so', I replied, totally forgetting the much-rehearsed 'yes Ma'am'.

The corgis followed her, and the Duke of Edinburgh and I walked among them, the pair of us side by side, to lunch in the 1840 Room. I don't recollect the names of the other guests: there were several community workers from Wolverhampton, the man who looks after the Crown Jewels and someone from St Paul's. It was very informal and the Queen, two seats away from me, joined in the conversation, asking questions that showed she had briefed herself well. The quiche, served on elegant china embossed with the Royal crest in gold, was superb, the best I have ever tasted – mine always seems to get lumps in it whereas this was just one lump of the same consistency, if you see what I mean. Beside the plates were four wine glasses of different sizes, again all embossed. I thought 'I'll have to do the business here. Drink out of all four of them'. This presented more of a problem than might be expected, for after the first glass of white wine, served from a bottle with a crown label on it, I felt I had drunk enough alcohol. I asked for Perrier water which was brought, then later for soft drinks, one of which was Coca-Cola. The butler said: 'I'm afraid we don't serve Coca-Cola, madam', and I felt I ought not to pursue the matter. Later a sauce was brought round for the pudding and I was embarrassed because I appeared to be the only person who did not know what it was. The Brigadier pointed out that it was brandy sauce and I said: 'No thank you, I'll give it a miss this time'.

After a little tour of the tapestries and paintings we returned to the morning room. There, to make my whole day, the Queen's lady-in-waiting complimented me on the dress that Minna, my dressmaker, had created. It was full length of beautiful midnight-blue velvet with black taffeta silk bows in front and white collar and cuffs. The Queen took up the remark and added: 'It really is very nice. Convey my compliments to your dressmaker'. Before we left, Prince Philip discussed the javelin knowledgeably – it turned out he used throw when he was at school. I was last in, last out, and on my way back to the Jaguar, the lady-in-waiting approached me and said that they were thinking of installing a small gym at the Palace. She wanted some exercises that would reduce her stomach. I told her to sit down and slowly bring back her head to touch the floor. Her eyes nearly flew out of her head.

Minna was having a busy time with me for only a month later, two days before my birthday, on 12 March to be exact, she provided a two-piece suit with the most spectacular hat – a neat little pill-box featuring the hint of a veil – for the MBE ceremony. I took my Mum and Dad with me, and Clement, and once again Carol did the posh chauffeuse bit in the Jaguar. The Buckingham Palace sentries recognised me, I am sure from their smiles, and there were a lot of photographs before we were sectioned off into knights, CBEs, OBEs and MBEs. The MBEs were last to go through and we waited for an hour and a half without a drink so a few old dears were nearly fainting. After a while, the Master of the Household came through to instruct us on etiquette – on reaching the Queen, the men should bow and the women curtsey, then after stepping forward, give another bow or curtsey before Her Majesty pins on a badge. Everyone was asking me what to do, as though I should have known from previous experience; I was worried enough myself, having made a right mess of the rehearsal. As we passed by Mum and Dad gave me big, proud smiles and I grinned back. The rest of our group looked very grave.

Waiting in line, a man behind gave me a little tap on the shoulder and it was my turn. I curtseyed well I thought, then smiled, then walked up and curtseyed again. 'Hello again, how nice it is to see you', said the Queen. I managed to remember my manners this time and replied 'Thank you, Ma'am'. She pinned on the medal, adding: 'This is for the honour you have given Great Britain at the Olympics'. 'It's my honour, Ma'am', I said. Then I curtseyed again and backed away, as you have to.

I was very happy. She was pleasant and in a champagne-coloured chiffon dress looked regal and self-possessed. The bandage which had been on her wrist at lunch was still there. Afterwards people said that everyone had looked so serious except me. I don't know if it was wrong to be cheerful but I can't see why it should have been.

No doubt in time the invitations will start to die out. Once I went back into training I had to cut out a lot of them but I am always anxious to help the Sports Aid Foundation which does so much for outstanding up-and-coming sportsmen and women as well as for established internationals. The chairman, Paul Zetter, has done a magnificent job with this voluntarily funded organisation. He and his wife, Helen, even 'phoned England from a holiday abroad to have a massive birthday cake made for me to cut at the Ambassadors Club. There is also, of course, the Variety Club, my chosen charity from a long time ago – their Sunshine coaches have helped so many disadvantaged kids. I always reply to letter-writers even if it takes a year. They have given me strength in bad times and if they can take the trouble I think I should, too. Just before Los Angeles, a 75-year-old man wrote to me from Birmingham saying he knew I wouldn't let him down; that I was going to win the gold medal. Then there was another, just after Moscow, who said I wasn't to despair, the darkest time is always before dawn. They helped, they really did. So although replying to 35 letters from one school, for instance, takes up a lot of time, I still think it is right that I should do so.

My rule of thumb on invitations when I am very busy is: will my attendance help and, if so, who will it help? This tends to mean that I go to old people's homes, hospitals and schools – I went round 18 of these to raise money just before the Games – and they leave a strong impression on me. Just after winning the gold I went to Carlisle Hospital and I hope it meant as much to them as it did to me when I signed little photographs and had chats. They made me feel like a superstar. My last call was to the old people and one lady started to cry. 'Thank you for bothering to see us', she said, and I didn't know what to do. I loved meeting the Queen but it wasn't as necessary as visiting Carlisle Hospital.

CHAPTER TEN

True Champions

There was Shirley Strong doing her outrageous act: wearing one of those tight leotards, swinging hips from side to side and blowing smoke from a cigarette. I was thinking that she was the perfect Coronation Street vamp doing that when, whoops-a-daisy, she bumped right into Princess Anne. Strongy clearly wanted to curl up and die but Princess Anne only raised her eyebrows a fraction and put on the faintest of quizzical smiles – she was ever so slightly sending her up and I had the feeling that she would have liked to join in the fun. She is that kind of character, on the surface apparently rather haughty, but, a little deeper, one of those people you wish you could get to know really well. I have met her on a number of occasions and each time I am struck again by her strength, rectitude, integrity and informality. She is one of those aristocratic ladies who discover they can help us all because they are born to independence.

At the Games she was Britain's special factor – incomparable as the head of our nation's representatives: a secret weapon. As president of the British Olympic Association, she took her duties as seriously as she does with the Save the Children. Often appearing at the trackside or in one of the sports halls, she visited just about every sport our country was involved in. I had seen her at so many functions where I had had a glass in my hand that when she arrived to sit between Seb and I at the Sports Personality of the Year dinner, she must have thought I was a stalwart drinker. We talked for a long time about racehorses, show-jumping, her home at Gatcombe Park and how difficult it is to come back after injury, something she experienced as an Olympic rider. Then Clement and I were invited by Jackie Stewart to a charity clay pigeon shoot at Gleneagles where I surprised no one more than myself by coming second overall. I was standing talking to Princess Anne who was there with her husband and we were laughing because one of the prizes was a monumental bottle of Moët & Chandon champagne. 'Whoever wins that,' I said, 'will need a tractor to take it home.' We chuckled and then listened to the awards. Second prize was, of course, this champagne, a Balthazar I learned later, prompting a delighted laugh from her. That is the story, I think, which amused the Queen.

It seems appropriate here, in company of the president of the British Olympic Association, to write about my fellow athletics gold medallists of the past two Olympic Games, Seb Coe, Steve Ovett, Allan Wells and Daley Thompson. Seb is the product of a close family, I would guess, and certainly at Moscow he was the athletics product of his father, Peter, a man with an original and even scientific mind, who was living out his ambitions through a brilliant son. I do not necessarily think there was anything wrong in that because Seb at that stage probably needed someone he could put his complete faith in and who better than his own flesh and blood. There have been criticisms that Seb was a 'manufactured' runner, whatever that is. I say that if it is possible to manufacture talent like that, why haven't the East Germans done so? No, Seb is a one-off, the records say the greatest middle-distance runner the world has seen. Just imagine what students will be asking in 20 years' time: Two golds for the 1500 metres, two silvers for the 800 metres? He must have been a genius. Well, for a genius he's a very nice man, neat as a pressed napkin and, at one time when he was overshadowed by his father, almost shy.

In Moscow there was about them a passion for success, almost a crusade, that I do not believe I have come across before. It was a two-man team with father the man who built the car and son the lad who drove it. Seb would talk quietly among friends and with the Press and you felt he wanted to be liked. By Moscow, the Press had dubbed Seb the good guy and Steve the bad guy – a stupid reaction based on the premise that Steve would not talk to the national newspapermen. He had his reasons: I know because sometimes I have wanted to tell them what to do with their typewriters. Seb was always available, Steve wasn't: or at least Seb's father was always available and wherever Peter went Seb was sure to follow. After the 800 metres, Peter said that a silver medal was not worth anything, it had to be gold. That is nonsense, try telling it to David Ottley and our men's 4×400 quartet. Peter was winding up Seb in pursuit of perfection but he might have been more subtle about it.

Between Moscow and Los Angeles, I came to know Seb better. He is a deep man and once he had cut away the tightest bonds from his father, grew to know his own worth. He realised, I think, that he was not competing for his parents but for himself. The lonely battle against illness must have concentrated his mind and by the time Los Angeles came around, Peter was in the background where a good coach should be. It is also right that a coach should be at your side and be able to understand you and, in fairness to Peter, he reached right down into his son's talent and took it, as completely as possible, into the stadiums of the world. Seb will always have far more to thank him for than to begrudge and I am sure he knows that. When the break came, too, it was made away from publicity, quietly and with dignity. Seb was suddenly, notably, his own man. So in Los Angeles we shared some marvellous jokes and it was a pleasure to see how those very different personalities, Coe and Thompson, got on so well. Seb went to the village early and stayed there, chatting to anyone who happened to turn up, dropping clues that the 1500 metres was to be his race at these Games, not the 800 metres which had always been regarded as his speciality. It seems amazing that he nearly missed his gold-medal event through non-selection, having been beaten by Peter Elliott at Crystal Palace. Peter, as I said earlier, is another of Wilf's gang and my sympathies were with him when he was omitted from the 1500 metres. I don't think the two of them should have been put in the position of believing that they were taking part in an Olympic trial – it was a publicity stunt that went wrong, the result of which could have lost Seb a gold and did nothing for Peter, who dropped out of the 800 metres with a fractured foot anyway. I shall make a prediction now: one day, and maybe not all that far in the future, Seb will be knighted, especially as he has become so busy with and valuable to national organisations. Arise Sir Sebastian.

I don't think that is likely to happen to Daley, especially if he carries on as a 'Hollywood Cop'. Daley is a peculiar mixture of selfishness and generosity, and I feel I can say that because I know him well and love him as a sister does a brother. To me, he is perfect. And I recognise that to others he can be an ogre. He appears not to care a hoot for anyone but those close to him know that often his wildness and bitter humour is a cover for the embarrassment he feels about having deep emotions. Daley should not have been cast as a Hollywood cop but as an Easy Rider, a supremely fit, don't-give-a-damn anti-hero. His practical jokes are legendary. He plays them endlessly on me, and one such was particularly smart. When we were on an Australian tour he promised to bring me a full breakfast in bed, me queening it with the best athlete in the world acting as waiter. Ten o'clock arrived and still there was no sign of the man. Then there was a knock at the door and shoved under it was a piece of dry toast, not even any butter. I opened the door and there was the butter and nothing else. He hasn't forgotten that one and I haven't forgotten that two weeks after splitting my Achilles' tendon he sent me a huge bouquet of roses with a lovely message. Do you know who he reminds me of? John Lennon. If you investigate their early lives, there are all kinds of similarities, even in the way they were brought up by doting aunts. Lennon just might have done what Daley did at the Los Angeles medal Press conference – debunking the affair with sly comments about Princess Anne as well as wearing the 'Is the Second Best Athlete in the World Gay?' T-shirt.

Allan Wells and Steve Ovett both met their wives-to-be through athletics. I don't know Allan at all well although he was on the Australian trip on which I became toast-mistress. We went to a disco one night, the only occasion on which I have really seen him let go of his inhibitions, and he was really funny. Margot and Allan have a profound relationship and now that they have a baby I am sure he will be even more of a family man. He is an obsessive trainer and is said to be a hypochondriac although I can't believe he is on the same scale as Lorna Boothe. She even packed a machine that stimulated the tissues of her leg. A walking medical box, that is what she was. I remember when I hurt my shoulder at a Crystal Palace meeting and every time I went to have it treated by a physiotherapist there was Lorna lying on the bed. In the end, I just gave up.

Steve Ovett's standards are those of a good man. If he's a bad guy then so was Francis of Assisi. He is an athlete when he is running and a kind man when he isn't – many athletes will confirm that when they were most down, Steve's encouragement meant a lot to them. He does not shout about his charity work or about the Phoenix Club he helped form for kids in Brighton. He goes silently about doing what he thinks he should. After the world championships, he knew how disappointed I was and said as he passed me at Helsinki airport 'Hello, Tess. Olympic champion loses – so it's back to the drawing board'. That put my defeat into immediate perspective because he had been beaten badly in what must have been the clumsiest major race he has ever run. The village buzzed with concern for him in Los Angeles. He was like a boxer who kept getting knocked down but each time struggled to his feet to carry on slugging. It seemed that way to me, but to his wife, Rachel, it was a mortifying experience. I was in the laundry-room of the British block doing my washing when she came in a few hours before the 1500 metres final and told me that the doctors believed Steve would be all right but he wasn't very well. For a while she really feared for his life. What courage he had, though. I sometimes wonder if people are aware of the integrity an athlete must have to become great. Out there, striving against the world's outstanding achievers, there can be no excuses for doing less than the best expected by the public. The public eye concentrates pitilessly on fallibility, and it takes men of rare moral courage, such as Ovett and David Moorcroft, to stand on the starting line knowing that they haven't a chance of winning because at that particular time on that particular day their fitness has been cracked by outside forces. It would have been easier and far less visible just to declare themselves unwell and sit in the stands.

I have sometimes been asked who out of Coe, Ovett and Steve Cram, all fully fit and at their supreme best, would win in a 1500 metres race. The records say Seb, because of victories over the other two in both Moscow and Los Angeles. You can discount Steve

Cram in Moscow because he was so young and also I believe that Cram was not race-fit in Los Angeles where he still won the silver. Ovett won the bronze in Moscow and, of course, dropped out on the last lap in Los Angeles. They have all had their share of world records. One day perhaps they will put all the evidence in a computer, as they have with world heavyweight champions, and come up with the best of them all. Not too many people would agree with my order, I suspect. It would be 1 Ovett; 2 Coe; 3 Cram because when it comes down to sheer cussed determination, and I think it would, Ovett would come out on top. I don't think he would have time to wave to the crowd, however.

None of these stars had greatness thrust on them, they had to bust guts for it. Seb's sessions are famous and while Steve Cram sometimes likes to pretend that his training is all very casual he does not fool those who know that to run his way means a lot of sweat has been left behind in Jarrow never mind the Grand Canyon. Each runner has an almost mystical telepathy with their coach or adviser, a kind of psychological bond between torturer and tortured that survives because they are inter-dependent and seeking the same rewards. Nowadays, Wilf Paish is not so much a father figure to me – there are some things I tell him that I would not dream of telling my father – he is a counsellor, even confesser and very much a friend. Most of all, though, he a guide to the goals I aspire to. I am a friend of Wilf's family and yet we all know that he has often sacrificed and given to me, and many others, what society may say he should have given to his own children. It is Wilf's choice. His dedication to athletics, track and field, cannot be bettered; further-more he is the man who can't say no, taking on as many as 20 competitors of differing quality and potential, diligently program-ming each until sometimes at training camp I have half-expected him to keel over with exhaustion. Three or four international athletes at the pre-Olympic camp in Lanzarote were slightly upset that Wilf was trying to coach so many who had no chance of going to Los Angeles that he left insufficient time to devote himself to us as we would have wished. His response was 'What have I missed out on, then?' and the truth was nothing, on paper, but quite a lot around the table with a relaxing drink in our hands. As national events coach he had been much loved and respected by athletes and it may, indeed, have been partly this that lost him the job of national director of coaching he so coveted. The decision in favour of Frank Dick broke his heart. With all due modesty, I think my gold medal was the biggest single reward of his life – it meant as much to him as it did to me.

But back to the torture chamber. Wilf and I practically lived in each other's pockets for a year. If either of us disagreed with the other we thrashed it out there and then, just as we had since 1978, a system that channelled off any possible bad blood. The weeks came and went with this sort of schedule: nine till one at Telvista; lunch; two till four at the track; four till six home for a sleep; six till eight training again. No weekend breaks, just one day a fortnight off.

Monday: weight-training. Heavy lifting, overarm work, bench pressing, leg pressing, squats, some of the disciplines in eight fast repetitions. My bench presses were up to 175 lbs, snatch about the same. Evening: bounding session 50 at a time; then different types, hop, step and jump; hop, step, step, jump; hop, step, step, step, jump; and further variations; five sets of five bunny jumps; bounding jumps; standing long-jump. In all, eight separate exercises.

Tuesday: Fast basketball and medicine ball work. These involved seven or eight different throws done in three groups of ten: about 250 in all, including overhead work, like footballers' throw-ins from the lying position, from positions on my stomach, from my knees. After that pulley-work. Evening: sprints, short drills, standing starts, 60-100-metre bursts, 150-metre repetitions of three (best time 18.06 seconds).

Wednesday: weight-training. Evening: more track work. Thursday: medicine ball training. Evening: bounding and sprinting. Friday: weight-training. Evening: multi-gym work. Saturday: alternatively resting or training. Sunday: javelin-throwing and drills. Evening: track work. In the summer this varied. Friday, for example, was a rest day if I was competing on a Saturday and generally the work was a little lighter.

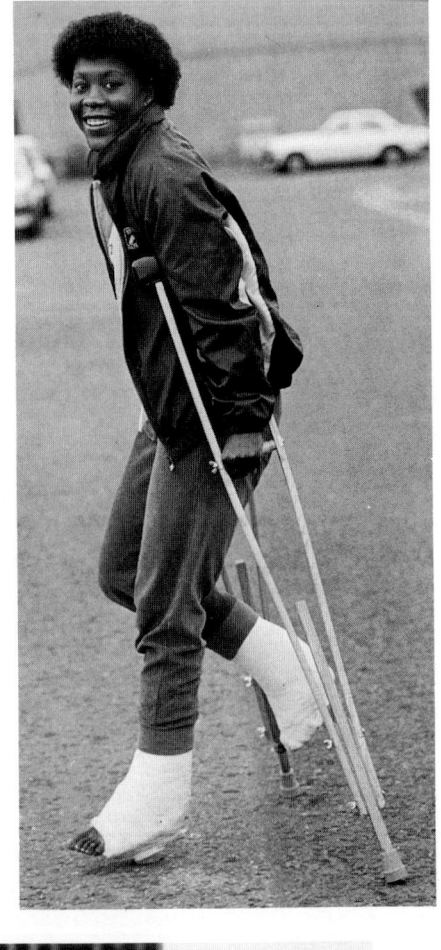

Right Double trouble as I heave myself away after the two Achilles heel operations; eleven months later I won the Los Angeles gold

Below This is the 1981 100 metres hurdles race in which I gave Shirley Strong such a fright; she had no idea I could hurdle so fast

Ruth Fuchs, the best javelin thrower I've ever seen

Miklos Nemeth, the coach who inspired me to win my Olympic gold medal

Fatima Whitbread; I have never doubted that she is a great thrower

Tiina Lillak, a friend whom I was delighted to see win the World Championships in 1983

Competing in an international athletics meeting at Gateshead in June 1985

A pinch of congratulations from Fats, though we haven't been pals for a long time

With Zola Budd. She's a pleasant girl but I don't agree with what she stands for

The year before Los Angeles for the first time in my life I enjoyed training. Brian had always said he wanted to fill out my five foot six inch frame to about 11 stones and I reached more than ten by the Olympic Games. Frankly, I didn't want any more. For all this period it was as if my mind had been taken over by a fixation. Wilf's schedules built me up and knowing that Miklos the Taskmaster would be clipping me round the ears in Hungary only made me more determined. When Seb said that some nights he could not climb the stairs after training, I knew exactly how he felt. That, however, I could cope with. More exhausting was having to haul myself around the kitchen cooking a meal because the coaches insisted I had good food every day. What a relief when Clement took me out for dinner once a week. In the mornings, I would have to grip my leg and throw it out of bed because my tendon was aching so much. Once showered and dressed, I knew I could walk the numbness off – then it was back into the old routine.

I don't think I could have done without Clement in Olympic year. He is very organised and concerned about making sure my life runs smoothly. I first met him in 1978 at a presentation in Leeds when he was with a crowd of footballers. He is rather suave, a bit of a dandy in appearance. I had practically forgotten his existence, and certainly his name, when he rang me in Telford to wish me a swift recovery shortly after hearing on *World of Sport* that my tendon had ripped. Once he explained who he was, I was touched by his thoughtfulness and also by how his voice gave away the fact that he rather liked me. Even so, it was two years before we were to meet again. I was staying with mutual friends, Winston Smith and his wife, Claristine, and after a training session one day when I was messing with their kids, Winston came in to say he had just rung Clement to tell him I was in town. Within minutes, Clement was at the house calling for me because I told him I was keen to see the film *Elephant Man*, which that he had been taking another girl to see. He seemed to have dropped her like a hot brick. On one trip to Wolverhampton – he buys and sells ladies' clothing – he called at Wood End Road, met my Mum, and promptly became my chief helpmate in the move to Leeds.

I was very cautious about boyfriends after Maurice, dedicating myself to athletics, and unwilling to face the possibility of another painful, broken affair. Clement, who is 35 and comes from St Kitts, was really aware neither of how serious my Olympic intentions were, nor even that I had won a Commonwealth gold medal. The man actually wanted me for what I was and not as a boast to his friends, a very positive mark in his favour. We decided to become engaged after the Olympic Games, put it back to St Valentine's Day which was then booked up by my visit to Buckingham Palace, and it seemed the right time would never come until I happened to be passing a jewellers in Leeds that was announcing 'Gold – Half Price'. On the spur of the moment I went in and an assistant called the owner, Michael Rossay, whose sales pitch was brilliant. I left the shop having ordered a diamond solitaire engagement ring my fiancé did not even know about: this was feminism gone wild. It wasn't even 29 February. I went up to Clement and said tentatively: 'Guess what? I've just ordered our engagement ring'. He just sat there laughing, couldn't stop. Wonderful man. He had his revenge though. The day after I received the MBE Mum, Dad and the two of us stayed in a hotel in London. I went up to my bedroom while Dad and Clement were having a drink, and there, in a little box in the room, was the ring. He hadn't even told me he had picked it up. I put it on at midnight on my 29th birthday. He's the best person that has ever happened to me and I think I'm the best that's happened to him.

CHAPTER ELEVEN

Poisonous Pen

Like anyone else in this life, I have behaved well and not so well. I know I have never actively tried to harm another person or to do anything that would make my parents ashamed of me. The story that I am about to relate makes me feel dirty, embarrassed and sorry for whoever it was that believed it was necessary to try to spoil what was the proudest episode in my career. It reflects badly, too, on people whom I don't know but who bowed to blackmail or, more precisely in this case, poison pen letters. I was the victim, the lady who was hanged without trial, and I did not even know at the time what the charge was.

Thames Television had decided that I was a suitable subject for *This Is Your Life* and so, totally unknown to me, the wheels began to turn with Clement organising who was to appear while all the time having to be careful I did not uncover even the slightest clue that the programme was being planned – difficult enough with an inquisitive devil like me around. Nevertheless he did very well and I was totally innocent of the likelihood of Eamonn Andrews calling on me with his Red Book. Investigations had reached an advanced stage – things had gone so far that they were trying to fix up an aunt's surprise appearance from St Elizabeth, Jamaica – when, suddenly, the whole plan was dropped and Clement, always a worrier and perfectionist, began to look so downtrodden that it was only a matter of time before he felt it necessary to tell me fully what had happened.

He asked me one night to sit down and listen carefully. He had wanted to keep the whole unsavoury business quiet but now he could not take any more as allegations were being made that could affect my life. This is what he told me. Early in January, he had secretly met in Leeds a woman representative of Thames Television's *This Is Your Life* programme. She stayed a couple of days while Clement and Wilf informed her of all she wanted to know, then she returned to London saying she would be in touch shortly. When she 'phoned back it was with a cryptic message that the television company had received a poison pen letter – actually more of a note with horrible suggestions in it – and that it was also being sent to my home. She was surprised because only a few people even knew the programme was due to be transmitted. They had invited Geoff Capes, Tiina Lillak, David Ottley, Fatima and were about to ask Seb, Daley and Edwin Moses along with various athletics officials. But no one, surely, who had this sort of grudge. Clement decided he had to intercept the letter and managed to do so on 11 January by standing guard at my letterbox.

He was very shaken. Eight days later another arrived postmarked Bow and, just as before, a copy was sent to the producers. The process continued for two months, the sole variation being that the first two were typewritten, the rest were produced by a person attempting to conceal his or her identity by writing with the wrong hand. They came from St Albans, Coventry, Cosford, Basildon and other parts of Essex. Meanwhile, Thames were putting off the programme time after time although they promised Clement that they would not give in to blackmail.

The early letters claimed that I had cheated my way to the Olympic gold medal by using steroids. Additionally, they said I had taken so many in 1981 that my tendons could not take the amount of training and had collapsed on me. I don't see that I have to defend myself against such insinuations so I shall simply say that I have never used illegal substances and have no intention of ever doing so. The writer's next revelation was that I had gained sponsorship from the six men of the Variety Club in 1978 as a repayment for sexual favours. It would have been laughable except that I knew the wives and families of several of these men who had gathered £2,000 every year for three years out of the kindness of their hearts. They are good, generous people and I shall forever be grateful to them. At this point, one letter became topical. Los Angeles police announced that Edwin Moses had been trapped while soliciting in a red-light area, an allegation which, knowing the man, could only have been absurd. The charge was dropped but my pen-friend said: 'I see your boyfriend has let his halo down. I hope he doesn't fall over the next hurdle when he comes over here'. Well, I did have an affair with Edwin when we were both completely free from other ties and, I think, a little bit in love. I still have great affection for him and for what he stands for in his gentle treatment of people and his belief in God and the power of prayer.

It was a long time, however, before I was to see this trash and even then it was a policeman and not Clement who showed the notes to me. One of them was out of character. It purported to come from an admirer and made sordid suggestions to me. People in the public eye are prey to this kind of crank but here there was a difference: the postmark was again Basildon and he wondered whether the originator was working at the behest of the original correspondent.

Clement had been so distraught that his doctor put him on sedatives and he was not helped by Thames's accusation at one point that he might have written them himself in some kind of fit of jealousy. On the other hand, he would have been less than human if the drip-drip of lies had not given him one or two doubts about my past. It is on such deception that evil people thrive. He seriously considered going to the police early on but was warned that investigations would reveal to me that I was to be the subject of *This Is Your Life*, and the show would be cancelled. So he soldiered on, relieved when Thames told him that the definite date for it would be immediately after my MBE when I would have received a lot of publicity. They went so far as to make plans to delay me in London after receiving the medal with the intention of springing Eamonn Andrews' surprise on me there. As the date approached, Thames received a letter which threatened that on the eve of the programme a national newspaper would be shown a document that confirmed I had been using anabolic steroids. It added that this would be their last *This Is Your Life* and would get zero ratings. Soon afterwards they excluded me from their plans and sent borrowed material back to Clement, although they claimed that the idea had been shelved only temporarily.

Clement thought they might have been worried that he had revealed details to me. He had not, although, of course, it is a risk they always take. Even when it was clear that Thames had made their decision he only skirted around the subject, mainly because he retained a faint hope that the producers would change their minds. Then he went to the police and, after they had seen me, the whole story poured out.

I rang Nick Whitehead, Frank Dick and Mary Peters. I was even warned not to sit by a lot of athletes in case one of them should drop something in a drink so that a later dope test would prove positive. Clement was so broken inside that for three weeks we did not see each other. I was angry and felt contaminated. When I thought of how Michael Samuelson and his friends had helped out of the kindness of their hearts I was gripped by cold fury.

Then we received a series of messages on my telephone answering machine. They were in a disguised voice, probably female, and gloated on every minor failure or mistake I had ever made. They continued through to the end of last season, generally after competitions and were related with undisguised glee when I had been beaten by Fatima. Two policemen questioned us at great length. We refused to speculate on who could have committed these despicable acts and left investigations to their professional competence. A number of people were questioned and the police went to the Home Counties and called on two women who denied any connection. There was an added reason for secrecy because I was due to collect my MBE and the last thing I wanted was to go to Buckingham Palace with these accusations around my neck. So we stayed silent and what should have been the most eventful, delightful period of my life was undermined by a guttersnipe. We just had to keep smiling. The police asked me whom I knew in the Basildon area and I replied that it was not up to me to make such guesses, it was their job to find out on the basis of real evidence. They said immediately that it was someone in the sport and that I had been the victim of professional victimisation by a very jealous person. The police even said that they had some idea of who it might have been. They made visits and gave their warnings but by then the damage had long been done and I can only sit back and think of what might have been.

So far no arrests have been made. That is annoying but in some ways the behaviour of the people responsible at Thames angered me even more. The programme would have been an enormous boost to me, a chance to say thank you to many of the people who helped me win the gold. A highlight of my life, really. The writer also knew this. Indeed, the writer knew a lot more about my background than a normal citizen would have. To Clement, it was a clue but one he could not use. There were others: the postmarks, for a start. Clement had checked *Athletics Weekly* for the dates of meetings and had discovered that the Warwick postmark was dated the weekend of a javelin squad session in Birmingham and that Cosford had been the scene of two indoor events at the time of those letters postmarked in the town. The writer really wasn't very clever but that did not make him or her any less vicious or vindictive and it was the evil master-stroke of threatening national newspaper exposure that, I am sure, scared off Thames. It was then that they cravenly withdrew, making excuses that the programme had only been postponed. I live with the fact that it will never be brought up again. What was less easy to live with was the possibility that they believed some of the trash written about me. Somewhere at Thames, too, there may be copies of those letters, a factor which could affect any future employment for me in television.

I considered brushing over these incidents when I started to write this book. It would have been easier to have made no reference and let time heal the wounds. But that would not have been right and in the long run counter-productive because I believe these people would be only too ready to re-start their campaign if they felt it necessary. Not only that, I have nothing to hide and, frankly, if I had I would still speak up because there may be other victims who are too frightened or sensitive to expose such blackmailers.

The writer had, however, revealed details that were self-incriminating. Undoubtedly the person had more than a passing

127

knowledge of steroids and was possibly in a position of some authority. First of all, it was news to me that steroids could lead to over-training and, consequently, great stress on the muscles and tendons; then another passage stated that I had had a positive certificate in 1984 which would be revealed to the Press. It would have been a forgery, I can guarantee. I was tested seven times in Olympic year, probably more often than anyone else on the circuit. Each time the result was negative, as I knew it would be. But the writer kept on pumping this misinformation into Thames. There could be no doubt that the letters were coming from a source in athletics and that this source was one of the few aware of my prospective *This Is Your Life* appearance.

I began to suspect all sorts of people and to become a little paranoid. Why was this done to me? I pleaded to Clement. I have always tried to be one of the clean people, working hard and honestly to achieve a great accolade. It was so bad that I started to avoid other athletes in case I said something that could be used by the letter-writer. I never suspected one of them; indeed I am positive that the letters did not come from an athlete. But a spot of gossip dropped over the telephone, a date here or a fact there might have led to more spite and vindictiveness – athletics at international level is a small, enclosed world. Clement now thinks he was wrong not to tell the police earlier for we ended up losing on every count. There seemed to be good reason not to, however, because of Thames's insistence. But the letters kept coming; I lost what should have been a memorable experience while the culprit must have been extremely proud of such a notable success by these most ignoble means.

I remember just how moved the nation was by Mary Peters' story on *This Is Your Life* and it had been a joke in our family that I had always said one day I would be on it. In a way, those chosen for it are people's champions and that is what I have always aimed to be. It is too late now. I shall never be asked to appear. A pity perhaps. But I have to say that if I was confronted tomorrow with Eamonn and his Big Red Book I should say, in most unladylike fashion, 'Get stuffed'. And here is a message to the person who made our lives a misery in the early part of 1984: I know who you are. And she knows that I know.

How would I like to have been portrayed, if it had come about? As someone who cares about other people, who comes from a good family and believes that you have to put in a lot of effort to be able, fairly, to take a lot out. I am no academic and I hate politics. People and friendship and warmth are what my life is about. And shoes and beans and waking up in the morning with a smile. Throwing a javelin has provided me with far more than a few medals and a strong body. It has whizzed me through doors, carried me scores of thousands of miles, brought me into touch with all kinds of characters – and I have found that the greatest communicator of all is laughter, brought about sometimes by my own loopiness. Appearing on *A Question of Sport*, Daley distracted me so much by pinching my knee that I answered his side's question. 'Virginia Wade', I shouted and the competition dissolved into joyous chaos.

I have several ambitions I should like to realise when I retire from athletics. Most of all, I should like to go and coach in the West Indies or Africa where there are dozens of people like me except that they have never had the opportunity or facilities to develop their skills. It would be a role as a sporting ambassador, showing kids how exciting athletics can be. I flew to Zimbabwe a month or so after Los Angeles, doing one or two lectures and trying to show children the rudiments of javelin technique. They were fascinated and I felt I had a serious vocation. Television is the other area that attracts me. I was always able to turn on the actress to some extent and now that I am no longer camera-shy I enjoy playing a part in *Game For A Laugh*, *Blankety Blank* and *Punchlines*. My favourite role would, however, be with children, preferably young teenagers with whom I very much identify. Perhaps the chance will come soon. Who knows?

In Olympic year there wasn't much time to do anything other than work, train, sleep and eat. I would just watch a soap opera like *Dynasty* and read some fashion magazines – I spend a fortune on clothes, sometimes with particular functions in mind but often because I find them impossible to resist. My taste in music is romantic soul, of the Gladys Knight type, and I'm really crazy about a reggae record I heard just after coming back from Los Angeles, 'It's Good To Have The Feeling You're The Best'.

I am no ardent feminist. In many ways I prefer men's company to women's, especially guys like the two Micks, Hill and Makins, who come out with jokes that few women, and definitely no lady, would dare even to think of. I feel that women often have a bad deal though; if they are doing the same job as men they should be paid equally. I went to a Woman of the Year dinner with the Duchess of Kent presiding over 300 of us, including Valentina Tereshkova, the first space-woman. It was all interesting but really and truly when I went outside I was longing to see and chat with a man. They are funnier.

CHAPTER TWELVE

Unwise Girls

It took many, many years for the line to be breached in athletics, for the massed ranks of officialdom to give way to the demands of modern-day competitors who know that to win at the highest level they must be supremely fit, sympathetically coached and tough-minded. Those qualities are not attained either by mollycoddling or by imposing rules for the convenience of officials: they come with maturity, experience and a degree of independence.

This is the era of the whistle-stop athlete, hopping like an American presidential candidate from jet to jet through long and, outside Britain, hot summers. The demand for javelin-throwers is not what it is for milers. How many miles, I wonder, did John Walker travel to run a century of sub-four-minute miles? My estimate is that he's on the equivalent of a return journey from the moon. Obviously I have covered nowhere near as much ground as that but I have more than done my share, reflecting from Furth in West Germany to Tokyo, Japan, on the astounding changes that have taken place since the line was first broken. Seb, Steve Cram and Daley will be millionaires if they wish to be and the fact that none of them makes it obvious that he does – and are genuinely, I believe, more interested in coming first than in plush homes and sleek cars – speaks volumes both of the character of British athletics and of the athletes themselves. Of course, they wish to be paid for doing what practically amounts to a full-time job. And it is right that the men and women who fill the stadiums of the world, and boost television audience ratings high into the top ten, should receive payments commensurate with their attractiveness to spectators and viewers. They are in show business as well as in sport: many officials may not

131

like it but it is too late now for the neanderthals of the stop-watch age.

By and large the British Board has presided over the track revolution with a faint sense of disgust and a great deal of mystification, depending on two or three men to guide them through the swirling mist. One of these, indeed the key man among them, is Andy Norman, whose techniques of applying pressure and getting things done say much for the Metropolitan Police, which he left in 1985 after 20-odd years having, it seems, written his own job specification as head of the promotions unit. Norman organises superlatively and, under fire, goes straight into the attack as he showed when he refused Olympic champion Joaquim Cruz permission to change a race at Crystal Palace. Not for Norman a quiet climbdown. Cruz did not appear and was further boycotted by others among the European promoters. That is a lot of power for a few men – these tribunes of the track – to wield and it would be, to say the least, unfortunate to fall out of favour with them. In Britain, Norman holds not only the key but the lock and the door as well, able with some ease to affect the quality of the IAC meeting at Crystal Palace last year, which was dimmed to a ghost of its former glory; unsponsored and barely televised. Cruz appeared but a number of renowned British athletes were missing. Later the IAC and Norman parties were to clash with a thunder that threatened to shake the AAA to its foundations.

Athletes are paid – although the Board dislike that word – by a system of subventions. Money is held in trust by the Board until beneficiaries retire, otherwise, we are allowed only training expenses and suchlike, basically to cover costs. Properly administered, there is much to be said for the system, my only strong argument against it being that the athletes themselves should have more say in the level of payments. In 1985 they were decided by the promotions unit, headed by Andy Norman, which would have brought vast problems if such power had fallen into the hands of the wrong clique. David Bedford, Derek Johnson and other militants of the IAC allege it already has. Certainly, it was lack of control over the supervisors of the money bags that led to the £95,000 payment to

Zola Budd despite the fact that she was thoroughly beaten by Mary Slaney in their first re-match over the Olympic 3,000 metres distance. Norman refuses point-blank to detail who gets what, although I understand the level of my subvention was leaked to some Press men, an act which I regard as outrageous. He has not yet to my knowledge spilled the beans on Fatima. Either subventions are secret or they are not.

Outside this area my concern is for the young men – I don't know of any girls of whom this is true – who have abandoned the chance of a career to become full-time athletes. It is a development brought on as much by difficulties in finding employers who will allow liberal amounts of time off as it is by the new payments system. Britain's number one sprinter last year, Lincoln Asquith, was forced to go full-time by circumstances that were also part of the reason for the Handsworth riots. Lincoln, 21 years old, lives in that area of Birmingham where more than 50 per cent of young blacks cannot find work. He says he is now a faster, fitter, better sprinter than he was – and moving into the prime of his life, so he ought to be – and yet his times and attitudes last season did not always reflect that. It was sad that a young man with qualifications in computer work was on the way to becoming an expert on day-time television programmes and just as well that he saw the dangers in that himself. Last autumn he re-enrolled for a polytechnic. Sprinters, unlike distance runners and field eventers, require in the main short, sharp sessions so they are rather more able to fit in with an office timetable. The real shame in Lincoln's case is that no one in the Birmingham area has offered him substantial assistance with a job or sponsorship. It will be no comfort to this intense, shy man that I found Leeds people much more accommodating in this respect than those in the West Midlands. Lincoln, Max Robertson, from Wolverhampton and Bilston club, and the growing numbers who risk going fully professional will inevitably miss out on much of the innocence and fun that I enjoyed in the decade up to Los Angeles. Banquets have been superseded by discos, leisurely build-ups by fly-in-fly-out schedules, serious intent by the solemn, grinding pursuit of records.

For the most part athletics is a clean, healthy sport, contaminated to a degree by drug-taking and to another by the behaviour of a few unwise girls. I was brought up to value myself and what I could give to others. I have had three boyfriends and dozens of minor flirtations in my life because beneath that bubbly surface is one very cautious, uncompromising girl whose trust has to be earned. Once or twice I have told myself 'I have so many friends I don't need any more', and while that may be true in some respects, it is ridiculous in others. Relationships are constantly being made, shifted and occasionally lost. My first boyfriend was a welder, Anthony Clacken, to whom eventually I became engaged. We were close for two or three years until athletics began to draw me away from him. He did not want anything to change while I dashed here and there, training, competing and attending functions, usually without him. Eventually enough was enough and after great heart-searching we split up. I knew there was little prospect of a fruitful marriage – he would have attempted to tie me down – and that he would be better off with a different type of girl. It was not until 1979, for a passionate year with Maurice, that I overcame reservations about a complete involvement. There were so many friends and distractions and, most important of all, I was not the girl for a casual fling.

I could not put Edwin Moses in that class, although later on I very much regretted the affair. Sonia and I were staying with Andrea Lynch and her husband, Brian, in California. Andrea had been displaced by Sonia as our number one sprinter but we were all good friends. It was the second time I had met Edwin and I was again captivated by his charm and manner. He went to endless trouble to visit me and show me around – I don't know why I should still feel a little guilty about it, but I do. Sometimes girls think they are having fun when they aren't. With Edwin I felt that we could have developed into a close and loving couple and possibly we would have done if the distance between our homes had not been 6,000 miles. He thought a lot of me and I did of him.

There was none of that about one lady who appeared to the public to be of impeccable virtue but was known to be otherwise among the men of the British team. It was this particular woman's aim to acquire a different man at every meeting, with a distinct preference for the heavyweights. She was insatiable, a nymphomaniac. The boys used to laugh about her and the story of her exploits at one international meeting became a legend. The guy she had chosen on that occasion set about trying to persuade her that as there was no beach near at hand, how about getting together in the long-jump pit later that night. She, I am told, was enthusiastic about the idea and was duly obliging him in the stadium pit when the lights went up. In a flurry of sand and underwear, the couple parted, dressed with as much dignity as they could muster and she, leading the way as though she had just won a gold medal, made for the exit. On another occasion, this same woman went home from a meeting with a scarf round her neck to cover a massive love-bite. Yes, she had a husband at home. Not surprisingly they have divorced since.

I am not suggesting for a moment that this is normal or acceptable behaviour but it goes on. It takes no imagination at all to comprehend why one teenager recently became known as Miss Seven-Up. The expression 'Did you score?' makes me shudder and each time I hear it from one of the guys I think how I would feel if I knew they were talking about me.

I have said before that Marea Hartman is, and must be, a sharp disciplinarian in these matters. At the Montreal Olympic Games where we had a particularly young team she imposed a 10.30 pm curfew and although from the way they dressed us it seemed we were regarded as a set of novitiate nuns rather than adult representatives of our country, if I had to decide I would prefer old-fashioned dresses and old-fashioned morals to smart costumes and lax attitudes. That goes for 90 per cent of the girls. The remaining ten per cent have to be treated with flexibility. Marea or any other team manager must say: 'The team's reputation is in your hands and any damage to that will lead to serious measures. If you must sleep in a man's bed, do it discreetly. And don't bed-hop'. There was an instance of that lecture to one girl recently who was collecting men like stamps. There is a middle way in these matters. I would hate a return to the days when they barred and shuttered the sexes away from one another – co-existence is the spice of life in camp. I know some people would like to see us behave as many in the Eastern Bloc do. At ten o'clock on a signal from an official, they all rise from whatever they are doing and head back, sheep-like, to the team fold. They win lots of medals, too. But I have been able to make significant contact with only one of them, Ruth Fuchs, in a long time on the circuit, an absence of fellowship that must mean the competitors from Communist countries are obtaining only half of what they should from sport. One of the great advantages of athletics is that at major games it allows people to mix freely and talk about anything and everything but their events. I am pals with competitors from all over the world: Filbert Bayi, Don Quarrie, Lee Evans, numerous Africans, some of whom almost adopted me as their mascot, the girl who showed that blacks could throw as well – not that they allow their own women to do so. I do not think I could name a black woman athlete from Africa. There must be some fabulous potential among the girls of Uganda, Kenya and Ethiopia, judging by the physique of some of them. The trouble is that athletics or sport does not rate among the priorities for women in these countries.

Our own girls are far more precocious – they know much more earlier than in my days as a teenager. One or two of them consider that away from the parental eye they must be game for anything, particularly once their competition has finished. This is what I call the post-competition urge, during which the girls often make the pace, as if to convince themselves that only by this ultimate personal experience have they enjoyed a good time. One of them will see the guy she wants and make sure she has him, regardless. I would warn any youngster that in having fun she should be careful about making herself an easy target. The buzz goes round very fast indeed. And if it reaches management level, when the next trip comes along the girl who messed about could be under a definite handicap.

Mind you, not all the officials are perfect. For a few of them, meetings are an excuse to over-indulge, usually amongst themselves but occasionally in a manager-athlete relationship. It's silly to be too censorious about this, for there are bound to be affairs where men and women are in close proximity. Managers should attempt, though, to control their feelings and provide no one with reason to accuse them of favouritism towards their friends. I have no reason at all to believe that Andy Norman and Fatima are anything other than warm friends but Norman's treatment of me last season fills me with doubt about that the wisdom of relationship. Can you wonder, when I see Fatima and her mother leading the way into a hotel while he follows, overloaded with baggage like some unfortunate porter? Perhaps I am doing him an injustice. If so, I can only say that the circumstances have provided reason for my suspicions.

Before I fill parents with alarm, I should say that most daughters understand only too well the price of being over-generous with themselves. Athletics itself is such a hard taskmaster that the girl who wants badly enough to be successful will usually know when the frolics should end, and will as often as not be advised by her coach of the pitfalls. Some, of course, have found good partners and married – Kathy and Garry Cook, Wendy and Les Hoyte, Bev and Clarence Callender, Sue and Colin Morley, Rachel and Steve Ovett, Margot and Allan Wells are among only the more recent. The Cooks have benefited tremendously from their love. They understand the demands the sport puts on each other and seem to have made the space in which they can survive and prosper. I knew Garry for many years as a fellow Wolverhampton and Bilston member and a cheerier, more gently humorous man you couldn't hope to meet. He is as talented a runner as any in this country, lacking only that final, arrogant streak that you must have to become a champion. Kathy, quietly, has more of it. I think they both recognise that. She is a real English lady, with steel.

From what I know of them, both Garry and Kathy steer clear of coaching each other. Most married athletes mention their training only in passing, perhaps occasionally asking for a word of advice but recognising that there are difficult waters to be traversed if, say, a husband tries to interfere with a coach's programme. Nevertheless there are couples who find they can complement the coach. Colin and Sue Morley are excellent examples. Wilf lays down the schedule but Colin is there for nearly all Sue's sessions. He has patience – so much of it I think he could even have taught her to drive! –and if one or two things do not turn out too well he will say 'OK, let's try again next time', and leave it at that. I have seen the other side of the coin where a husband really let the wife have it from the hip. 'What the hell do you think you're doing?' he would shout and she would just quiver each time. That one ended in divorce.

I have had an extended relationship with one athlete, Maurice, and that was enough for me. Conversation can be limited to only one main subject – what time you did, how well you jumped, how many reps, what you lifted – and the monotony grows until boredom creeps in. Sometimes you need to expand your knowledge of one another, not contract it. I could not even contemplate spending long with someone who was interested only in athletics, especially as I am not a facts-and-figures girl. With a few exceptions, I cannot even remember my performances, let alone those of foreign athletes. And, of course, there is the constant problem of knowing only too well what male athletes are like. Hardly one of them does not believe he has special attraction for the ladies – and many of them, it is true, are exceptionally fine looking – so there is the matter of trust also. Whether a girl allows herself to be used, or becomes a type of athletics groupie, is, in the end, entirely up to her.

One of the guys off the scene now, Gus McKenzie, had a funny experience during the European junior championships in Duisburg. A crowd of us decided one night to visit a bar called the Gaslight. Gus, a friendly sort, was soon deep in conversation with a German whose offer of a drink was accepted. Within minutes Gus was heading for dreamland. Suddenly we realised he had been slipped a Mickey Finn and that this friendly bar was, in fact, a gay bar. Fortunately we had one or two of the big lads with us and they pulled Gus away from his drinking partner and led him, tottering, back to headquarters where he went out like a light.

Athletics abounds with characters. From Steve Green, the scruffiest athlete I ever saw, and the Tancreds, through Geoff Capes, who I called my Big Daddy, to Mike MacFarlane, Donovan Reid, Brad McStravick, Daley and my two Micks. We have gone into bedrooms – often with me the only girl – sat down, played cards, had a laugh and behaved perfectly. Most of the jokes would not have passed muster at the Palladium but it has all been harmless talk and horseplay.

When I was in my teens, the Tancreds, who were also in the Wolverhampton club, used to frighten me. Their jokes were so rude and they were so boisterous that I felt small, innocent and vulnerable beside them, which I suppose I was. One day they invited me to a party at the Crystal Palace hostel and, always game for a bit of fun, I asked them where it was to be held. 'Our room', said Peter. 'We're having chips and a blue movie.' They were, too. I made my excuses that time. There were lots of warnings not to get mixed up with the big boys, but although they would twang my bra, pinch my bottom and even turn me upside down and shake me until my stomach was ready to drop out, they were also very protective towards me. I think I became their little sister. The Tancreds were legends, you may think, for all the wrong reasons, yet I don't agree. They were mad amateurs who competed because they loved the sport and its freewheeling atmosphere. They invited some of us to skinny-dip at a meeting in Nice. I had no idea what they meant until they reached the beach and pulled off all their clothes. They ran into the sea. I ran the other way.

Yes, I do have sympathy for the youngsters coming through now. Will they one day regard athletics rather as workers think of the factory or clerks the office? The British Board ought to be looking into the possibility of scholarships or placements for athletes of exceptional ability who cannot find jobs. Perhaps they could extend the subvention scheme to cover education or re-training, at least a productive use for the 10–15 per cent they take from all of our earnings. This is all the more necessary because the days of sponsorships for all but the very best competitors appear to have vanished. I was very lucky with my six helpers from the Variety Club. Michael Samuelson was filming a meeting in Dusseldorf for the IAAF when I happened to impress him with a throw. He was also struck by the fact that I was wearing a big Union Jack on my chest, so he introduced himself. On the flight home we began to chat and I told him that I was being held back by lack of finance, a condition that was not helped on this trip because my company were not paying me for time off. He couldn't believe that once off the 'plane I would have to cart my javelins through the underground on to the train from Euston and then on the bus home. So my marvellous new friend decided to do something about it. He organised five other men to pay into my bank account a total of £6,000 over three years up to Moscow 1980, the only proviso being that I sent a postcard to each of the six gentleman friends from wherever I was throwing. I still do so. I became very close to Michael's daughters, Emma and Louise, spending weekends at their home where I became part of the family. The three of them were in Los Angeles and watched my event, Michael because he was working on the official film, Louise because she was helping Emma, and Emma because as Emma Samms she plays Joan Collins' daughter Fallon in *Dynasty*. Fate has a funny way of arranging coincidences.

Financial help during a key period of an athlete's development should be the Board's priority long before they chuck money around as they, and many other national associations did, on Carl Lewis. Every precaution must be taken to prevent the sort of money-go-round that is beginning to haunt athletics. Lewis openly sold his golden talent for pieces of silver last season, running when he was not properly fit, being prepared to lose races and not giving the public their money's-worth. His crude, ostentatious pursuit of wealth turned off sponsors during Olympic year and his discovery that the four-gold hero of Los Angeles was not as marketable as he expected clearly perplexed him.

I believe athletes should be paid according to their merits. But how much more satisfying to remember an old fellow of 90-plus who came up to me after I had opened a children's art gallery in Leeds. He said he had made a special trip to say hello and tell me what a wonderful girl I was. I gave him a kiss, showed him my gold medal and signed a picture. Then we had a gentle hug. Those few moments confirmed my faith in what I believe to be the true value of athletics, way beyond money.

CHAPTER THIRTEEN

Fighting Prejudice

I am extremely proud to have been the first black woman to have won a gold medal in a throwing event, just as much as I am proud to have won the first throwing gold in British history and to have been only the fourth British woman Olympic champion since the Second World War. Before I am British, black or even a woman, I am a human being and it is only on this that I would wish to be judged. Nevertheless being black gives me a special responsibility, for I do feel that there is prejudice against my colour and I do feel that I should speak up about it. There is a unique vantage point in athletics, too, because it is the only sport – and I suspect the only area of life in this country – from which the shackles of racialism have been more or less cast aside, partly because performances are measurable in time or metres and, therefore, assessable in the simplest terms. Anyone suspecting that they have been turned down for a job because of their colour will be aware of the problems associated with providing proof that this was so, even if the black person's qualifications were equal or slightly superior to those of other candidates. Employers may simply say that the winning man or woman was a better person for the job in other, non-quantifiable areas whereas in athletics, the black sprinter who has run faster can clearly be seen to be the best man. More than this though, blacks and whites actually blend encouragingly well in the teams, so much so that often I describe people without reference to their colour which is obviously their most visible characteristic. I do not think I have ever outside my sport been quite as elated as I was when a *Sunday Express* poll among readers found that I was the most popular woman sports personality in the country – it proved to me the potential for fuller integration and the goodwill among readers of what is, after all, a Conservative newspaper.

I have spent all but eight of my 30 years living in a predominantly white society and it is inevitable that I have shared many happy times with whites, probably in athletics far more than with blacks. And I have friends in mixed marriages whose love has endured. Whether I would marry a non-black is a different question: I think not, but for practical reasons and certainly not racist ones. I have known couples who are dating fall out and in the end the boy or girl has turned round and said 'You black bastard' or 'nigger'. I am no silent wallflower but I do not think I could stand the hurt of that – not from someone I thought a lot about. I have developed a protective shell about certain things and this happens to be one of them. Yet I am enough of a realist to know that people fall in love for any of a thousand and one reasons and I suppose the shell could be cracked.

At present, as I said, you would have to grub around very hard to find any prejudices in British team selections and even harder among the athletes who know that when they are on the starting line waiting to go all considerations other than who is fastest are forgotten. Assumed racial superiority must be pretty quickly re-assessed when the rival next to you flies off to victory. This is the Jesse Owens factor. Hitler would not countenance Owens' explosive, invincible talent, not from a poor black whose gifts diminished his own countryman's. To millions, Owens lit a torch for equality in Berlin, the citadel of facism. What irony! An historic accident, maybe, but epochal because there, in the moment that Hitler refused to acknowledge Owens' victories, the disease was highlighted and re-identified to the democracies of the world. The Olympic Games can never have a finer hour. I felt the Mexico Black Power salutes were a useless charade in such company. Although I understand why Tommy Smith, Lee Evans and John Carlos felt they should make them, they became a token of something else: a deliberate, sinister plot to introduce politics into the Games.

Many years ago I admired Angela Davis, a freedom fighter now practically forgotten. I thought she was indomitable and that I would carry the same standard through life. When you look around, however, you discover prejudice everywhere and not just colour prejudice either; bias in class, intellect, politics, and religion is just as widespread. As a black in daily life in Britain, one rule must, however, be constantly borne in mind – you need to be 150 per cent right to win your case. Prejudice breeds in the unlikeliest places. You learn not to go looking for it, but it can be impossible to avoid. I was asked to start a charity football match by kicking off at The Hawthorns where West Bromwich Albion play. As soon as Cyrille Regis and one or two other black players came out they were greeted by opposition fans as 'monkeys' and 'gorillas'. Apparently it happens quite frequently that supporters make ape sounds and even throw bananas. I think I might stick my javelin into anyone I caught doing that to me. My feelings about mobs of fans who make Nazi salutes at black footballers are unprintable, as are my views on the National Front, whose advocates travel thousands of miles to abuse black players in their own England team.

On an infinitely smaller scale, I was caught up in a situation which I believe was caused not so much by prejudice as by the fact that, as a member of the black minority, I was not representative of the public at large. I was among three sportswomen on the shortlist to advertise Clark's footwear. I sent pictures of myself and my mother to them, hoping to win a useful contract, but finally lost out to a tennis player who was barely in the world's top 50 and whose name was unknown outside a few of the game's enthusiasts. It was explained to me later by a friend how impossible it would have been to recommend to clients that an advertising agency should use a black person as representing the shoe-buyers of Britain. I was not the right image. It is hard to accept that, although I know exactly what problems they believe they would have had. If I was really bitter I could say that I became wholly acceptable in Britain for only a short while after winning the gold medal. Yet I know that decision made for Clark's was perfectly understandable in business terms: shoe sales could have been lost. It would have set an excellent example, however, if a big firm like Clark's had had the courage to knock down a barrier.

Excuse the pun, but few matters in life are black and white. I know the problems of inner-city areas: massive unemployment among younger people; frustration at poor housing conditions; uninspired schooling and poor facilities for sport and pastimes, but it is wrong to react with violence. It is wrong, too, to go to war with the police over conditions that they did not cause but must control. The police have a tough job to do and the great majority do it without fear or favour. Some are prejudiced though. They do stop black boys without good reason, I have seen it happen in Wolverhampton, and occasionally they rough them up. On the other hand, some of the boys who rioted in 1985 were, I am sure, manipulated by drug-pushers.

Where prejudice exists, it must be confronted and fought vigorously. Many black people are too passive about this. I say that if you feel you are good enough, get in there and challenge for a job or for your legitimate rights. If there's a vacancy, apply. Be brave and keep going for the line. There will be plenty of hurdles, I know because I faced them and I am facing them still, but you have to be bold. I am largely optimistic about the future, partly because in sport black people have proved themselves the equals of any other race. That has given us self-respect and made others respect us. I am proud to have played a small part in this breakthrough – to have been able to line up with famous black competitors who shadowed Jesse Owens. From the time I was first surrounded at the Christchurch Commonwealth Games by Africans who said they had never seen a black thrower before I have been aware of a particular kind of responsibility, to my race as well as to my country.

There remains one exception to my optimism: South Africa. While I disapprove of boycotts, in the case of South Africa I support sanctions to the hilt. Exclusion from competition has exerted tremendous pressure for change in the system of apartheid which cynically divides a nation by the colour of its people's skins. In many ways, isolation from sport is more effective than trade boycotts, unless these can be taken to their ultimate. South Africans can grow their own food and produce their own goods at low prices subsidised by the cheap labour of blacks and coloureds, but they cannot escape from solitary confinement as a nation without international friends in art or sport. I would not compete in South Africa for all Oppenheimer's gold and I have no respect for any black person who does. He or she is worse than a mercenary – he is a Judas. I have heard such people make the excuse that they perform in front of predominantly black audiences but we all know what happens when the audience goes home. They are back in their segregated townships where oppression rules and police shoot indiscriminately. Although I do have sympathy with blacks there missing out on major sporting spectacles, they generally accept that this is one of the prices of future equality. There may be others, much dearer. The pressure must not be relaxed, either. Competitors who go to South Africa to earn tainted money should be made aware that they do so without the approval of the Commonwealth and should be excluded from the Games. I also believe that national associations should refuse to pick these people.

Rugby presents an enormously difficult case because the national unions are not answerable to anyone but themselves and are able, for instance, to ignore the Gleneagles Agreement which puts a Commonwealth seal on sanctions by sportsmen. Rugby's ties with South Africa are close and subtle, partly because rugby is rarely played by black people, but chiefly because it is supported, as is cricket, both by state money and big business. It seems unfair to me that the Commonwealth Games should suffer boycotts by African and Caribbean nations because of the refusal of one sport to recognise the obscene realities of apartheid and the consequences of upholding it. On the other hand, if rugby ransacks internationally-framed sanctions, other sports attracted by the pickings may well try also. It is a dilemma for the black athlete to know what to do. I am, however, prepared to take a stance in a fully-implemented boycott should English black athletes decide that it would be useful. As a woman who likes to think she is self-reliant, I hate this kind of 'strike' but the cause is big enough, mark my words.

It is the non-Olympic sports through which the South African authorities can best work at undermining the sporting blockade. The problems with the England cricket tour of the West Indies in

1986 showed how conscious the rest of the world has become of an issue that unites the black nations in detestation of apartheid. I have some sympathy with players who spent the winter in South Africa coaching youngsters and playing in inter-state matches. I have none at all with men such as Graham Gooch or Peter Willey who secretly negotiated with the South Africans and then sold their services against the advice of the MCC to tour with an English representative side. That was despicable. Gooch and his grubby band were banned from Test matches for three years. I don't think that was anywhere near long enough but at least it was a start and showed official disapproval. It may seem odd that I support Gooch's right to refuse to sign a statement vowing he will never tour South Africa again. However, a person taking such a stance must accept the repercussions that are bound to follow and, even more to the point, so must the selectors who pick him. West Indians were legitimately entitled to make their feelings known by protesting peacefully and by boycotting the matches.

But cricket's blemishes are small compared with those of rugby. The home unions were not invited by South Africans to tour as the Lions in 1986 and I think one of the major reasons was that there would have been national boycotts of the Commonwealth Games in Edinburgh. The Scottish union would hardly have been very popular causing that and so a real breach has been made into the stonewallers of the game. No doubt there will be many moves yet. The Australian cricket rebels' tour that winter proved that the South Africans are alert to every possibility of making mischief. The pressure to abide by sports sanctions increases year by year, however. If there is another national rugby tour of South Africa, it will start such a rumpus that it will certainly be the last. Unfortunately, it could also lead to another games boycott, victimising the very people, like myself, who most agree with the fight against apartheid. I would like to see someone organise an Athletes Against Apartheid movement – I'm not sure the AAA would enjoy having the same initials – to crusade among people whom the general public respect and would generally follow.

Which again brings me to Zola Budd. As I wrote earlier, I like Zola and became good friends with her in Los Angeles where she was clearly very lonely in a strange and sometimes hostile environment. She was the child of a marriage of convenience between the *Daily Mail*, who paid her £250,000 or more, and the British Government which actively assisted her in queue-jumping by hurrying through her passport while hundreds of others less fortunate were forced to pass through all manner of processes before acquiring one. This was opportunism of the worst kind, motivated by thoughts of nicking a quick gold medal. Would a black athlete or, say, an average South African runner have been similarly treated? Of course not. I have little doubt that Zola's advisers saw ways of making big money out of her, a theory reinforced by her demand for £95,000 to run against Mary Slaney. She is an immensely promising runner, potentially the best long-distance woman the world has yet seen, but the chance she represented of a medal for Britain should not have been allowed to outweigh the efforts of other girls who at short notice found their Olympic hopes in serious jeopardy. The irony was that one of the threatened girls, Wendy Sly, won a silver medal in that historic 3,000 metres final.

The point that distresses me most about Zola is that she has never denounced apartheid. It was utterly wrong of the GLC to make threats about withdrawing aid to athletics if she would not do so, and I support her in not bending to that moral blackmail. I wouldn't have done so myself in the same circumstances. But at some time, if she understands the rights and wrongs of morality – and unquestionably she does – she should let us know her opinion of the apartheid laws. It was noticeable in Los Angeles that she made friends mainly with the black girls and someone remarked to me that she appeared more comfortable in their company, perhaps because at her home in Bloemfontein she had been brought up among them. I do not know about that. It only struck me how much she liked the sense of humour and comradeship among the whole team, who all felt terribly sorry that her first Olympic Games should end in the shock of being booed around the track.

When she first came to Britain, some of my friends wondered whether she regarded them as slaves. We were all extremely wary of her at first and, because she was surrounded by such an entourage, few of us had the chance to make any contact with her at all. I thought the demonstrations against her were stupid and, in the case of the council banner hung at Edinburgh, counter-productive. She cannot be held responsible for the situation in South Africa and it must be hard for her to criticise her country when her parents and friends live there. I suspect, however, that she has come to learn that it is perfectly easy for black and white people to live together on equal terms. If she has discovered that, I think it would be of enormous benefit to harmony in sport if she declared her hatred of apartheid. Although she has dodged its sporting consequences and made huge sums of money by doing so, that is immaterial if not unjust. Her friends on the team would like to hear her views. I think she owes that much to the country for whom she competes and, more importantly, to those who know right from wrong.

CHAPTER FOURTEEN

Fatima Whitbread

In any chat I have about athletics, the questions about what it felt like to be Olympic champion will sooner rather than later be followed by: 'How did you get on with Fatima?'. I find it impossible to be impartial in my answer just as I find it hard to separate my relationship with her from our respective relationships with her mother, Margaret, until recently national javelin coach, and Andy Norman, manager of the national athletics promotions unit. Unquestionably the most powerful man in the sport in Britain today, Andy is a special friend of Fatima and Margaret and during the Olympic Games the three of them stayed in the same hotel while most of the rest of us settled happily on the UCLA campus in Los Angeles. That was their business. For my part, I preferred to spend my time with friends who helped make the hours speed easily by. Fatima therefore missed out on one of the most important elements of big competition: the comradeship that comes from knowing you are among people who are shortly to face great trials with all of their character and ability. Being on the same wavelength has a profoundly relaxing effect on most of us and I do think Fatima would extract more from the sport if she switched on to it. It seems to me that Margaret has cocooned her and potential friendships never materialise because people are not permitted to come close in the first place. Certainly the other athletes would like Fatima to join in more often, and I found early in her career that she could be good fun – she has a bright sense of humour. That was when we shared accommodation once or twice and the general crowd of girl athletes welcomed her as a potential champion who would be a long-term colleague and chum. At about this time, Fatima had a personal problem her mother was trying to sort out. This was upsetting her

149

so much she even talked of giving up athletics altogether. It is ironical that I wrote to her pleading with her not to stop and pointing out that the two of us could make Britain the strongest nation in the world in women's javelin. That at least has come true.

I admire her as a thrower. Her aggression ripples through a 13-stone frame that has been built up by, I am told, incredibly tough training schedules in and around the purpose-built gym she has at home in Thurrock. Technically her standard is good although I believe that when I am at my best my throwing has more co-ordination than hers. It is bulk acquired over the past three years that has given her the thrust to throw within a metre or so behind my British record last season when she openly boasted that she would score a grand slam of javelin titles: the Olympic, World, Commonwealth and European. It is just possibly that she will, but besides having to deal with Felke and Lillak she should not be kidded by her five victories over me in 1985 into thinking that I am a broken reed. We shall see this summer.

The answer to the question about how well we get on is that we could never be close friends – neither could Coe and Ovett – and so we both consider it sufficient to say 'hello' before a competition and 'well done' or 'bad luck' after it. Until last season in a match at Birmingham I felt no animosity towards her, a little antipathy perhaps but nothing more. It is fair to say I was niggled in the build-up to the Olympics because my chances seemed to diminish in the eyes of the Press and athletic authorities as hers correspondingly increased, yet for all his prejudice Andy Norman at least had the sense and decency to help provide training for me with Miklos in Hungary. Relationships rarely stand still and I suppose Fatima's and mine descended from a plateau of toleration towards one another in the year or two before the world championships in Helsinki. Objectively, I do not know who to blame for this, although I suspect Margaret set me up as a target to be beaten by her adopted daughter. Fair enough, many a parent does this sort of thing, except that when such a parent happens to be the national coach – and one, incidentally, who had taken over from Wilf, my coach – many difficulties can be created unless the official concerned has particular powers of justice. Margaret did not remotely possess these.

It was she who cut a ridiculous figure in Helsinki by storming into the British Board team room demanding to know whether 'Tessa Sanderson has a room of her own'. I have to admit that I like a private room unless there is someone I am comfortable with. In Finland, and in common with the rest of the team, I happened to be sharing, my room-mate being the kind and gentle Welsh lady, Vanessa Head. Margaret, presumably frustrated by her failure to catch me out, headed out of the village in a fury, demanding to speak with Andy, for whom I could feel only sympathy: the policeman's lot is not always an 'appy one. The upshot was that the Whitbreads were provided with hotel accommodation and, again, were welcome to it.

Fatima produced one marvellous throw in the Olympic stadium, Finland, dragging it from her boots after a qualifying round that would have depressed many a less confident and proud competitor. I was glad that she helped to show Great Britain was a javelin force to be reckoned with in the inspirational home of javelin-throwing although, to be honest, I was even more pleased for Tiina to take the gold. Later the repercussions of Fatima's silver medal made life so uncomfortable for me that I wonder what indeed might have happened had she struck gold. Andy appeared to be conducting her business affairs for her, a situation that actually did not occur to me until on several occasions fellow athletes pointed out how close their relationship was. Then I began to understand the implications of Wilf and I on one side ranged against Sergeant Norman, Mrs and Miss Whitbread and, as I became a little obsessive about this London connection, concerned with the official coaching set-up, too. After all, Frank Dick, the national director of coaching, and Wilf were not on speaking terms. What a political mess of potage. Fortunately, it also became clear to me that Frank was not the man to let a coaches' feud interfere with his job of producing medal-winners.

By some coincidence, the Alexander Stadium, Birmingham, has been the scene of two of the worst personal clashes between Fatima and I. In the 1984 prelude to Los Angeles, I showed that I was no spent force while being careful not to reach my best too early and thereby leaving good impressions in Bolzano and Belfast, only to fail – once again my so-called reputation was hounding me – on the big day. It suited me perfectly well that Fatima was universally accepted as Britain's number one for it meant I could train quietly at Carnegie away from the expectations that are heaped on any competitor in our country who is considered to have medal chances. Maybe for a showgirl like me the lack of attention was overdone, for the British Press treated me as though I had a communicable disease so silent were they about my prospects. They plainly shared the Board's view that I was not among the elite that could be expected to bring glory back home. Anyway, I just got on with the job as never before, knowing that I required one early Olympic qualifying throw and then a good level of competition to keep me simmering. Fatima had beaten me by 6 centimetres at Crystal Palace on 13 July and then, with many misgivings, I was inveigled into competing in Birmingham two days later. Why I always comply with smooth-talking promoters, I'll never know.

Rain was sweeping from the motorway side of the Alexander Stadium and all my fears of further Achilles' tendon injuries surfaced as I stood, dripping, among the puddles beside the track. Early on I threw a fairly respectable 62.54 metres and thought 'come on, girl, it's time you weren't here', and sensibly opted out, thinking I had done my bit for the drenched fans. Fatima threw 67.14 metres, an admirable distance in that weather and one she must have been pleased with. I went up to her and said: 'Well done, Fatima, you handled that well because the conditions are really bad'. She turned round and with a deep cut in her voice said: 'If you think 67 metres is only a good throw, you don't know what a good throw is'. I was so shocked that I replied: 'I feel sorry for you, I really do', and walked away.

This was a minor disagreement compared with the bristling track-side row we had on 6 July 1985. It would have made much better television than the actual contest, a two-day match with East Germany, won with spectacular ease by Petra Felke. Billed as the ultimate shoot-out – ITV's response to the BBC's screening of the Wimbledon men's final – our guns were spiked by the current world record-holder whose fast and stylish throws reached as far as 72.82 metres. Fatima was second with 66.30 metres, and I was third with 64.80 metres while Tiina Lillak, a specially imported guest, was a pale imitation of a great thrower, coming an abject fifth. It happens – Tiina will be back, as she showed when she beat me in Finland later in the season.

In the weeks before the competition, Fatima unwisely commented that it was bigger than the Olympic final and that she would be up there with Felke. I thought that her performance had upset her when, looming towards me like a night-club bouncer, she shouted 'Oy, I want to talk to you'. I said: 'Not now. I'm just going to say "well done" to Felke because she's just thrashed the hide off both of us'. Eventually, I went over and asked her what the trouble was. 'You know', she said. I hadn't the vaguest idea what she was talking about, but she carried on: 'You keep going round saying things about me and I'm going to have you for defamation of character'. I still hadn't a clue about what she was getting at. 'I've got good lawyers and people around me and I'll get them to sue you', she continued.

'What do you mean?' I asked. Very agitated, she said: 'You've been on TV saying I've been taking anabolic steroids'. I denied it and walked off, saying 'I won't come down to your level', at which point she made a very unladylike comment, telling me to 'f... off'.

The officials around us were boggle-eyed at Britain's two star javelin-throwers being involved in such a confrontation. I have never been so embarrassed in my athletics career. To try to put the incident into context, I thought back to what I had said in the Yorkshire Television programme a few weeks before to which Fatima must have been referring. I had been questioned about my preparation for the season and how I thought competitions with Fatima would go, then the interviewer had asked me about why athletes were looking so much bigger these days. I said something about how much harder they were training and he veered into another question about Fatima. 'Could she have thought I was alluding to drug-taking?' I wondered to myself. Obviously. But if it had been that clear, surely she would have sued me – it would have been a terrible and insupportable slight on her character. My anxious walk took me to the side of the stand where I saw Andy Norman hurrying towards me. From there he had observed our furious conversation and wanted, in characteristically blunt language, to know 'what has the silly bitch been saying to you?'. I said: 'Andy, I am fed up with this and if you don't sort it out there's going to be a lot of trouble'. By now, Clement was beside me and seconds later we were joined by Margaret Whitbread. She stated angrily that I had accused Fatima of taking drugs and that, as a result, they had been receiving nasty 'phone calls. Then she claimed that Clement had sent the police to her home in Thurrock as part of the investigation into the poisonous letters I had received. We denied this. If the police went there it was purely on their own initiative. In great distress, I explained to Daley what had happened but did not take his advice to tell the Press as I felt I could not take any more fuss at the time.

At the presentation half an hour afterwards, Fatima tried to make amends by chatting with me. However, the situation wasn't going to be solved as simply as that, and she must have known it because later on when Andy came to my room for what we hoped would be a meeting to clear the air, he admitted that I had not accused Fatima of taking drugs. I also told him that I believed him guilty of favouritism towards her and although we came to a sort of agreement the result was not productive. Andy Norman is a peculiar mixture of thoughtfulness, ruthlessness, cunning and generosity. Not even his greatest admirer would call him charming and yet he has risen to the heights of British athletics by utilising his brilliant skills as an organiser and 'Sergeant Fix-it'. He is also, I think, a man's man, abrasive and conspiratorial, whose experience trampling through the AAA has made him a few friends and a number of frightened enemies. But at least he has always supported the athletes' cause. No less a judge than Steve Ovett says in his autobiography: 'Andy has done more for the sport of athletics in a decade than most people achieve in a lifetime ... He is the architect who redesigned and shaped the sport – in Britain and to a certain extent internationally – to fit more closely with the present-day needs'.

No doubt that is true. But it does not excuse his bias, as a senior Board executive, towards Fatima, which goes far beyond official concern that British team members produce their best at major events. This was manifested twice in Los Angeles where Andy, an impressively ample man, was spotted watching the qualifying and final rounds. I was warming up for the qualifying competition and smoothly delivered a throw of somewhere around 67 metres: even Wilf, wearing his Matias Prats disguise, was pleased. A bystander remarked that I was going well and was amazed to hear Andy comment that I wouldn't throw like that in the final, I never did.

My Olympic victory was clouded by another incident. As I walked from the tunnel, euphoric and with images of the medal ceremony passing through my mind, a friend of mine involved with international athletics abroad pointed out Andy, Fatima and Margaret making for the bus. He said: 'Be wary of that man, he didn't want you to win tonight', and added that Andy had been jumping up and down shouting 'Come on Fatima, get in there!' and 'Get after her!' to such an extent that my friend thought Andy was going to have a coronary.

I decided before the 1985 season that, rather than dealing with my finances myself, I would find an agent. Andy did not like the fact that I wanted him to deal with the International Management Group, with whom Seb is also a client, and before my first competition decided to take things into his own hands. As organiser of the trust fund, he is entitled to do this but I was still surprised when one day he appeared at Carnegie in Leeds during a training period to discuss my scale of payment. This money may be used for training and other athletics expenses with the remainder going into trust with the Board until the athlete retires. Andy said he wanted to settle matters there and then, offering me £1,500 a meeting which was about the same or marginally above what Fatima was to receive. I thought the differential in favour of an Olympic gold medallist should have been greater and added that he should talk about it with IMG. Never a man to let advantage slip, he retorted that he would knock a third off if he was forced to go to an agent. Talk about a Sergeant Bilko – Andy Norman has all the qualities. Eventually we came to an amicable settlement, but I wondered who briefed the press at a Gateshead meeting that I was on £4,000 to £5,000 a time and wasn't prepared to turn up for less. Not true on either count. As I said before; I was prepared to declare my earnings, if everyone else did the same. Indeed, I think it right that people should know where the money in athletics is going.

This season women javelin-throwers are involved in the grand prix which seemed chaotically-based in 1984, its inaugural year. It is ridiculous that a man such as Steve Scott could win the overall prize for 1500 metres without ever having won a race. However, I know that Andy had a good deal to do with the system which at least ensured useful sums to athletes in what, immediately after Olympic year, is usually an anti-climactic season. He has done an enormous amount for competitors although he sometimes rules by fear, bullying them, for example, into taking on meetings for television when they would have been better advised to rest. In many ways I respect him and his bluster does not frighten me, either.

I have little respect for the third member of the anti-Sanderson trio, Margaret Whitbread, a woman who, it seems to me, would go to unreasonable lengths to support her daughter's cause. I have heard her talk openly of throwers who, she alleged, were taking anabolic steroids. During Olympic year she made spiteful statements about David Ottley, one of the most affable athletes in the sport, but a Thurrock man who had walked out on her because of his dislike for her character. She said he would not make the Los Angeles team, a forecast which undermined her stature because, of course, David not only made the team but also won a silver medal. David, Peter Yates, Simon Osbourne, Steve Pearson and almost every other male British thrower of any standing wrote to the Board asking them to replace her as national coach soon after the world championships because they felt she was interested only in Fatima's performances. This was not done, I believe, because someone at the Board felt it would look odd if the mother of the world silver medallist were sacked so soon after the Games. Then a second letter was forwarded to the Board, one that most of the girl throwers also signed, and again it appeared to be ignored. Perhaps this collective vote of no confidence had some effect, however, because Margaret resigned towards the end of the season and I cannot help remarking that nothing became her so much as her leaving. I think Margaret exerts a tremendous influence over Fatima and while we all accepted that a mother would and should have special affection for her daughter, she has gone far beyond that. When Wilf did the job, he was everywhere, helping everyone and with no favourites so far as I could see. Wilf's talents ought to be used as widely as possible but it seems that increasing alienation is leading him to other areas and countries where they are more appreciative of his dynamism and obsession with every form of athletics.

As for Fatima and me, there is no chance of patching things up. We have gone too far in opposite directions and, anyway, we have very different and uncomplementary personalities that are epitomised by the way we throw: Fatima is uncompromising, broad and strong, the thorough professional; I am less confident perhaps, more precise as a thrower, smaller, faster, dedicated though not to the extent that she is. I will give her a few words of advice, however. By boasting about 'grand slams' and how she will beat the world she only puts pressure on herself and might make herself look ridiculous. The odd thing is that she has avoided the slur that stuck for so long to me, that I would be all wrong on the night. Fatima failed to win the Commonwealth gold she expected in Brisbane in 1982 – she ended up with a bronze – was not placed in the Europeans that year, did well for a silver in the worlds and, from the pronouncements she made beforehand, must have been grievously disappointed with the bronze in Los Angeles. Last year, the only time she came near Felke was in the World Cup in Canberra where she threw 65.12 metres for Europe to the East German's 66.22. Unfortunately for both of them – and amazingly in Felke's case – they were both beaten by Russia's Olga Gavrilova who managed a lifetime best of 66.80 metres in a swirling wind. Apparently Felke was so distraught that Fatima had to comfort her. I do not know if anyone was in the Australian capital to comfort Fatima for if her grand slam is to become a reality she will need to take advantage of such situations. Personally, and without prejudice, I do not think she is anywhere near good enough. I will buy Andy Norman the biggest lunch of his life if I am proved wrong.

CHAPTER FIFTEEN

The Drug Scene

I have never taken drugs. My view, simply, is that I have never wanted to win by cheating and drug-taking cheats not only your opponents but yourself as well. Besides that, there can be no way of knowing what damage may be done, short- or long-term, especially important to me as I wish one day to have a family. Yes, I have been accused of swallowing anabolic steroids to help me train harder but the source of that calumny is one for whom I have no respect who has now been removed from our sport. Apparently, this person volunteered to a reporter friend of mine at a meeting in Birmingham the misinformation that my throw was illegal because I was on drugs, adding that I would refuse a dope test. As it happened, I did have a test and it was, of course, negative.

A year or two ago, a well-known former international thrower said he believed 60 per cent of the British team had at some time used drugs, specifically steroids. I would not like to guess the proportion but from my observations I guess he would not be too far out. The drugs are easily available and the temptation for an athlete who knows that rivals are taking them has to be very great indeed. My own position is that in a dozen years as an international athlete I have seen only one of the pills and that was on a foreign trip when a javelin thrower showed it to me. I laughed at him. To think a little pill could do so much, it was ridiculous. I am not naïve about this, however. If I wanted to go on a course of steroids they would be available within hours. The people who push them are well known and even if they weren't it is possible to acquire steroids by perfectly legal means. Now, however, I know I don't need them. I won my gold medal without resorting to cheating and that means almost as much to me as the achievement itself. It was important that someone who looked as feminine as Tiina Lillak or me won in Helsinki and Los Angeles. Hundreds of kids, and their coaches, can be confident that it is possible to beat the world as a javelin-thrower by fair methods.

It would be a lie however to say I was never tempted to take what so many of the other girls did, especially after 1977 when my Dublin victory over Ruth Fuchs influenced me to believe that, with the proper treatment, I would consistently challenge her world status. As season followed season and my progress in reducing the gap between us remained infuriatingly slow, this temptation grew and was indeed increased when Eastern Bloc throwers suddenly began to reach distances that we all knew were beyond their technique. They broke records by brute strength – the shooting stars, I called them. Here today and gone tomorrow, but if they could peak at the right time there was every chance they would steal medals from those who acquired fitness by endurance.

There were two Ruth Fuchs: the one who broke world records and the other who appeared afterwards, slimmer, her voice several octaves higher, a very feminine lady, as an official with the East German athletics teams. The first manifestation, 12 stones or so, hard-looking with a deteriorating voice-box, was the woman who in Dublin could not register that I, a nine-stone three-pound parcel of skin and bones, had beaten her. She seemed to think I had discovered a secret potion that turned a weakling into a superwoman. 'What medication do you take?' she half-croaked to me. Neither she nor the East German coaches believed my protests that this was just me, unaided by stimulant, booster or pill.

By this time Wilf had advised me of the tell-tale signs in a steroid-taker. The neck bulges, sometimes a kind of acne appears, particularly on the back and face, the skin pigmentation changes and, if the drug is inexpertly administered, the patient sometimes blows up grotesquely. There was no other description to suit Anna Verouli, the Greek woman who won the European championships in her home town, Athens, in 1982, and was banned in Los Angeles for illegal use of steroids. I could name others whom I am certain indulged but the law will not permit it. I had a special regard for

Ruth because her talent was immense and, like Petra Felke, she is among the most personable of Eastern Bloc athletes, who overcome official dislike of communication with Westerners to prove they are not robots with fast legs and no personality. Ruth, amazingly aggressive on the runway – she uttered an agonising Jimmy Connors-like grunt as she delivered the javelin – became so much a friend that she would pop into my room for a chat and the loan of my hairdryer. Such communication blows open even iron curtains. She escaped from the terrible consequences of looking like a man-woman. I hope she always will.

Brian Newman convinced me that strength built up over the years would be more than equal to the burdens inflicted over shorter periods on those who choose to take steroids and thereby train with an intensity that the normal athlete cannot match. There were other reasons, too. I do not know how I would ever be able to explain to my family that I won meetings and medals by fraudulent methods. If my willpower were not strong enough, then I know that I would have their confidence, and that of my coaches, to lean on. How do the authorities stop drug-taking? As with all crime, it is easier to provide an answer on paper than to enforce the rules in real life. However, a start has been made on the twin solutions: certainty of detection and consistency of punishment – but only a start. In Britain we have led the way in trying to root out the wrong-doers, even to the point of testing at inter-club matches. Many of us feel there has been a degree of unfairness in this because other countries have not so much punished offenders as encouraged them, finding ways to avoid detection so that competitions are often not between one person and another but between the clean and the dirty. The best answer would be the random testing by incorruptible, impartial examiners of any athlete at any time in any part of the world. Maybe this will come one day – the cost would be enormous, even to the wealthy International Amateur Athletics Federation – but I suspect even if it does the pharmaceutical industry, either deliberately or inadvertently, will find a way round it by the discovery and manufacture of new drugs.

Increasing rewards for winners compared with losers is bound to put even more pressure on competitors to break rules. That is why punishment for drug-taking should be very harsh. At present, the IAAF ban an offender for life and then give remission after only 18 months. This is crazy. It is almost an invitation for athletes to try to beat the system the IAAF has set up. Marti Vainio, found guilty after winning a silver medal in the Los Angeles 10,000 metres, can expect to return in time for the European championships this year despite all the lying and prevarication that went on as he tried to wriggle out of punishment. Detection of anabolic steroids is practically impossible three or four weeks after the last dose – which makes you wonder how he was silly enough to be caught – and, presumably, Vainio could have trained on them all last winter knowing that he was safe from further tests. A gold medal at the European championships in Stuttgart or the world championships next year in Rome would soon help him forget the loss of his Los Angeles silver.

I say that punishment should be for the period stated, that is life. Until athletes know they risk their entire careers, and with the growing number of full-time competitors that would be a severe penalty indeed, they will continue to circumvent the system. If athletics politics do not permit the hard-liners to force through such a policy, then the smallest possible effective ban would be for four years, while perhaps the International Olympic Committee could also take action by banning Games offenders from the next Olympics four years later. In the end we are not dealing with law-breakers but people whose desire to win is so overwhelming that they are prepared to risk future health, even life, for the sake of a medal or much, much less. They have to be protected from themselves and, in the case of those from countries who collude in drug-taking, from the ruthless people who do not care about anything but their own prestige. So, although in one respect I think our performers and meetings have been unfairly selected for special attention, in another I am full of admiration for the British pursuit of integrity and for a man such as Sir Arthur Gold who has harried drug cheating at the cost of his own popularity.

There is a seductive view among athletes, propagated recently by Steve Ovett, that drugs should be permissible provided they are not lethal. Steve reckons that if you can't catch all the drug users then why not recognise the fact and allow those substances which can be shown to be less harmful? This, of course, begs the question 'How harmful is less harmful?'. Worse than that, however, it is rather like saying that if you can't catch every thief why not let them all go free? No, the rule must be that every athlete should be certain in the knowledge that he is competing against opponents on the basis of fitness, talent and intelligence, and not also on the use of banned drugs.

The dangers of a drugs free-for-all are horrific to contemplate. I am plagued with the thought of medical parallels such as the unknown effects of a substance as apparently harmless as asbestos. Men and women are still dying from contact with it. Thalidomide is an even better example. Here was a wonder-drug to assist pregnant women which proved to be the agent of fearful deformity in many babies. There are unscrupulous coaches even now who feed their athletes with illegal substances. Imagine what might happen if someone decided to experiment on guinea-pig athletes. All right, so that thought should be left in nightmares. But the obsession with winning leads to all kinds of excess. In one respect, however, I do believe that athletes are not being well-served by doctors. Sometimes officials react by reflex against anything new and possibly uncomfortable. If we are prepared to put our trust in authority to make good rules for us then that same authority should keep us fully informed in this case with straightforward details of which drugs are banned and why, and what the possible after-effects are.

Of all the British field-eventers, I reckon I have been selected for most dope tests. In 1978, I remember about eight of them. At one meeting the team doctor, Dr Andrew Matthews, stood almost embarrassed before me. 'Oh, God, it's not me again!', I said. And it was. I had to wee in the bottle so often I could have set up home in a toilet. I weighed ten stones at the time, a stripling compared with some of the hulks out there. In 1983, I was tested after every competition I had with Fatima. 'Don't tell me this is random', I said on one particular occasion. Fatima appeared to be luckier and was hardly ever called on to fill the bottle. It was no bother, really, except at one Crystal Palace meeting when I had to fill myself with Coca-Cola before I managed to eke a drop out. Much, much worse were the femininity tests that are in the past now but once were so degrading that they put some girls off competing. It felt like a cattle-market when first, as a junior, I was told to strip down to bra and knickers for a woman to prod my bust and other places to make sure I wasn't a man. Today, many of the girls look more masculine but officially are not, having passed the far more civilised saliva test.

Athletics has no bigger issue than drugs. The inner circles echo with rumours of who's on what; on wonder nostrums that make Olympic champions out of also-rans; on where they can be acquired and from whom. There are advocates of a controlled system and even a few of ceasing control entirely. To those misguided people, I put this question: where does it end? And once even the smallest barrier falls, competitors will pour over it. That is human nature. My principle is this: may the best man win. Not the best drug. True fitness is wonderful – God's gift to this century, I call it. Whether you are nine or ninety, the possibility of good health through exercise has come within easy reach. I would like just to touch on a few of my experiences which will help people to feel bright and lively.

The routines for an international athlete would, I am sure, kill rather than cure many people. I do, however, have total belief in weight-training as exercise, an opinion confirmed by numerous sports people who now use weights to improve condition accurately where once it was rather a hit-or-miss affair. There are cowboys around the fitness studios but find a trainer of good repute and I can guarantee that a month's programme will change a slothful creature into someone with a new zest for life. Jogging has had its detractors but I am not one of them, provided that if you are elderly you do not overdo it. The idea is to trot nice and easily for a mile or so, taking deep breaths and pumping your arms every six strides or so. For goodness' sake, though, don't exhaust yourself going red in the face and out of breath. I have seen middle-aged joggers pounding on for

164

mile after mile. I know they enjoy it and see long distances as a challenge but I think it can cause stress. This advice comes from experience because I ran fitness classes in Wolverhampton when Bob Hazell and George Berry opened their club. In one class I had 27 older people, most of whom wanted to shift weight from their bottoms and thighs. They were great fun and at first giggled when I made them lie along benches with their bottoms at the very end and their hands over their heads. They had to bounce their feet from the floor to their chests: that was one for the stomach muscles. This is hard enough if you're unfit – much harder were the sit-ups, the straightforward method of lying down then taking the hands from above the head to the feet. Later one or two did it from an inclined position, head below the level of the feet and then the same motion. Simple squats, up and down, look easier but aren't after a few of them. The grunts and groans from all of my class were terrible to hear, but the pupils kept coming back for more.

CHAPTER SIXTEEN

Throwing for Money

Athletics showed signs of over-indulgence in 1985 as the 'spend, spend, spend' mentality bloated some people's sense of self-importance and left others wondering why the more fortunate competitors were offered salmon and caviar while others were expected to survive on dry bread and water. News of Zola Budd's £95,000 hand-out, leaked to embarrass British Athletics Board officials, did far more than bring blushes to competitors as widely varied as Olympic medallists and humble joggers: it sent shock waves reverberating through the system. Waves that will continue to slow-fry a few reputations.

The responsibility for this gross over-payment has been well concealed but, whoever attempted to wriggle away from admitting actually making the decision – and if it was not agreed by Andy Norman in his capacity as head of promotions, then it should have been – there is no hiding its implications. It means that one or two officers were beyond the control of the Board itself. The payment was a symptom of many other ills and the comparison between Zola's sudden new wealth and the banning of a boy for winning a bag of sweets in Scotland was well made. Both were grotesque parodies of democratic decision-making. I prefer, however, to use a different example to the ten-year-old boy's unhappy experience. The problems of 20-year-old Phyllis Watt, a Birmingham auxiliary nurse, last winter were similar to the ones I experienced a dozen years ago. Four nights a week she travels by bus and train to Wolverhampton where she is picked up by her coach. After training at Aldersley Stadium, the journey is reversed, and she is deposited late at New Street railway station in Birmingham before she makes her way across the city to her Handsworth home. Following that routine, fitting travel and hard training into the corners of one's life, is designed to make even the most dedicated athlete wonder whether it is all worthwhile. Maybe such processes do sometimes toughen up youngsters with the will to become champions but far more often they will put off young people, and particularly girls who, in their later teens, are vulnerable to scoffing pals and boyfriends who prefer that they go to the pictures or a pub and who, most of all, are affected by the high cost of travel on public transport. It takes a particularly single-minded girl to overcome these obstacles, to stick at it in the often false hope that their determination will be rewarded by medals, glory and occasionally even money.

Phyllis has big potential. For years she played around with training for the 400 metres, turning up when she felt like it until she matured sufficiently to realise that either she had to give the sport a go or get out altogether. Many others just drift away, talented but unappreciated, marry and have kids. Thousands could have been subsidised by the money Zola was handed that night she came fourth to Mary Slaney, who must have been furious when she heard that she was paid £40,000 less than the then 18-year-old South African. I was very lucky that there were several people around who refused to let me while away Sunday mornings in bed, who made special journeys to take me to Aldersley and to competitions. Not everyone, however, has a Barbara Richards or a John Walker to urge them on, give them the fare home, or to encourage them and sometimes curse them for being idle, nor for that matter a John Moogan to coach them so sensibly.

As a field events competitor, there is another aspect that concerns me: despite the large amounts of cash that are required for coaching the jumps, vaults and throws, British officials are allowed to throw away money that national coaching director Frank Dick said equalled half his entire budget. Running may be more attractive to spectators and I do not decry the track competitors, except to say that most of them have a relatively easy life. The technical events demand highly efficient skills as well as natural ability and as they also have a beauty of movement far beyond the mere moving up and down of arms and legs, it is time television directors began to do a proper job of camerawork on them. Seb was probably right when he claimed early this year that in 1985 there was not a single field event shown in its entirety.

I do not criticise Zola for accepting the £95,000, although asking for it was a bit of a cheek. The Board should have laughed her out of court but instead they gave her the money. On reflection, maybe it wasn't her demand at all; maybe it came from her advisers, who have guided her career with sly skill from the turbulence of her instantaneously-provided passport, through Olympic misery, her own desire to give up the whole charade, into the world cross country championship, the 5,000 metres world record and a shower of riches. The South Africans not only have an outstanding competitor for their own deprived sports-lovers to admire, they also have a wedge to press into a multi-racial society and to twist to order. It must provide hours of amusement in Pretoria that we are paying for all of this. Britain has Thompson, Coe, Ovett, Wells, Cram, Sanderson and Strong and, while none of them has ever received to my knowledge more than £20,000 for one appearance, between them ABC TV and the Board paid five times that amount to a girl who came fourth. Someone, somewhere is crazy. No wonder a new system of checks has been imposed on the promotions unit.

The storm that broke over British athletics will take years to dissipate. The ante has been upped and the negotiating positions of Norman and his colleagues have been significantly weakened, as the 1984 AAA annual meeting exposed. The athletics clubs want more of a voice in determining the future of a sport which they nurture through good times and bad. The AAA has been forced to recognise this and have made changes in the structure of their general committee which may help to control excesses. Andy Norman, Nigel Cooper and Marea Hartman were not around when I was so short of money that I couldn't afford a Wolverhampton vest. However, the marvellous Bob Roberts, club secretary, was, and it was he who pushed the vest into my hand and told me, with a wink, that I could pay in my own time. People such as Bob deserve strong and fearless representation to help them to the top by the most direct route.

The question I cannot duck is whether I would have accepted £95,000 had it been on the table. First of all, though, what were the chances of such a sum being negotiated? The answer is nil, or less. Indeed, the clamour would have been so loud that it wouldn't have taken six weeks for the news to break – the time it took for the Zola payola to become public knowledge – but about six minutes. My name would have been hauled through the newspapers in rip-roaring headlines proclaiming my greed. It took only a couple of weeks for my alleged payments to appear in print as it was. That made me very upset. However, should some crazy man offer £95,000 for one competition, I would ask what damage it would do to the sport and what damage it could cause me. Depending on the replies, I would refuse or accept although the temptation to take it would be enormous. That is why I don't blame Zola. Competitors should not be put under such pressure, anyway. The example of tennis ought to have provided sufficient warning of that. Before the Association of Tennis Professionals took action on the control of the sport by a few players, the system was in chaos, with tournaments being held to ransom by the biggest stars. For a while this ceased to be the case but the problem is surfacing again, this time even more dangerously because the players' agents are in command. Other sports are being affected, too, as well as athletics. Agents vary from being indispensable to being necessary evils but they should not be given the power to do anything other than negotiate payments and conditions for individual competitors. I think the public would be horrified if they were fully aware of the deals that have to be struck between event organisers and agents, some of them with the clout of multi-national corporations. The Olympic Games themselves are not immune.

Athletes, as I said before, are by upbringing, experience and often nature inclined to be selfish people whose tendency to be suspicious of others cashing in on their hard, usually lonely work saves them from chasing the fast buck without considering the consequences. Every top exponent I ever met has two qualities: understanding that there are no short cuts to success, and love of his or her event. Generally, once the reserve is cut away, these qualities make them nice people and certainly fill them with humility, for failure stalks every competition and will even, unbelievable as it may seem, catch up with Edwin Moses one day. I know he will be ready. Agents, then, are not so readily welcomed, for surely no competitor will ever ask for direct reward when major games medals are at stake. This is significant because once a competitor accepts that she has to be at her peak for a particular event, the whole season must revolve around it; consequently the performances either side of what I call the 'magic month' will be below one's very best – and selling second best is not all that easy. I believe, though, that current difficulties – and there are a growing number of them – would be eased by paying mainly for performance. That would mean straight prize-money, so that the incentive to win and therefore to compete in prime shape would be enormous. Fat appearance money not only blunts appetites, and I say this despite the £10,000 I was offered each time I competed in British Board meetings this year, but it also leads to a distortion of values, angers other competitors, and puts power into the hands of manipulators and middle-men. Laughably-entitled amateur athletics should come out of the closet and declare the necessity for a proper professional system, clear and above-board, with winners taking most. What appearance money there is should be distributed strictly on the basis of the previous season's world rankings, on four-yearly cycles of past results and with a smaller allowance for the entertainment value of the person or event concerned. Figures for each athlete should be calculated by an impartial group of three or four experts and be announced in grades at the beginning of each season. The first grade could be for Olympic, World and European champions, world record-holders and athletes in the world's top three; the second for Commonwealth gold medal-winners and winners at all major games; and so on right through to, say, AAA and WAAA finalists. The system agreed for 1986 is an improvement on the secret deals of 1985 but still something of a lottery and a charade. Begone trust funds, subventions and backhanders! Begone, too, the thick mists which hide £95,000-payments to young, half-proven girls from hateful regimes!

And back to Zola: as I said earlier, I think I speak for every black athlete in the British team when I ask her to pronounce against apartheid. The crudity of the GLC attempt to blackmail her into doing this appalled me, but the point was not thereby invalidated. I accept, too, that she is a competitor rather than a politician and that she would be regarded as a traitor by many white South Africans, perhaps even by those closest to her, if she spoke out against such an evil. But it is an evil, and by her silence she gives comfort to the perpetrators of a system whose law says I am not as good as she is. Nor, it says, is Daley. Nor the rest of those black people who would like to be her friends. She has, ironically, been accorded the sort of privileged treatment in Britain that whites are used to in her country. I think the authorities should once and for all stop molly-coddling her, allowing her to infringe rules – there are several cases of blind eyes and deaf ears among officials including, to my amazement, the usually impartial Marea – and bring her totally into the context of the team. Most of all I want to hear her say that she believes in equality no matter what the race, creed or country of a person. Then I will regard her as what I, an immigrant like her, am proud to be: British. By a simple reckoning, Zola must have made something approaching £400,000, maybe rather more, from two years in this country. Seb should by now be near to millionaire status while Daley has had so many sponsorships, projects, advertising contracts and now a Hollywood television series, that he need never again back-flip on to the landing cushion – mind you, he will. Of all the British Olympic gold medallists, I suppose I have come off least well and, in order to improve my finances, which were looking sickly, I signed a promotion contract with the International Management Group, on Seb's recommendation. They have done magnificently for him – for me they earned less than £2,000 in a year. Shortly after winning in Los Angeles I set up a small company to try to exploit my success, eventually signing with Mark McCormack's group the following January. I entertained hopes of a solid sponsorship, probably based on endorsing equipment bearing my name, and working for one or two major companies and appearing on television – all to allow me the freedom to train regularly and perhaps to enable me to draw out a useful sum from my trust fund on my retirement a year or two later.

IMG's fee for their services was 25 per cent of all work and ten per cent of my athletics subventions (the money paid into trust funds from which only training and other expenses may be drawn until retirement). Time went by and so little work came my way that I wrote to Mark McCormack, who asked that I should be patient. Brad Hunt, the representative assigned to work with me, left, but still practically nothing arrived until, fed up with the whole business, I arranged a release from the contract which was granted amid apologies. Looking back, I think I was too unimportant for IMG. They seem to be able to help such celebrities as Seb Coe and Selina Scott, but for someone trying to move up the ladder they were a waste of time. And, what was worse, I missed out almost completely on potentially the best year of my career from an agent's point of view. The search for a major endorsement continues, leaving me mystified as to why I have been singularly unfortunate. At one point I asked Brad Hunt: 'Is it because I am black?'. He thought not, but I am inclined to believe otherwise. To put it a little crudely, I am not ugly, I have an outgoing personality and I am not stupid. So what other reason could there be?

I now realise I was wrong to take IMG's advice on another matter. Because I did not train at all until January 1985, and knowing that the season was bound to be an anti-climax after the Olympic year, I wanted to miss it altogether, returning a year later to compete in the Commonwealth Games and European championships which I particularly want to win. IMG persuaded me otherwise with the result that I suffered five consecutive defeats by Fatima, who admittedly threw with great consistency, and hardly enjoyed the summer at all. Although my best throw ranked me fourth in the world, I know that my reputation was dented. The only experience I really enjoyed was winning the TSB Golden Girl award, the prize a magnificent £2,000 brooch, for producing the outstanding performance at the WAAA championships in Birmingham. That brought the old smile back. I bridled at all the defeats, pride rubbed raw at any ability to do much about them. Gradually, my deepest competitive instincts rose to the surface and by September I knew I had to concentrate on recovering my Los Angeles level of fitness. As my heel pains receded, so I stepped up my routines, visiting Miklos in Hungary for a week every month or so. Wilf was away on coaching stints abroad for much of the winter and I was grateful to the two Micks at Carnegie – Makins arrived at one session with a pair of knickers on his head – for their advice, company and humour. I longed to train for the heptathlon but Dr Durie said this would be a mistake despite the fact that my heels were firm under heavy testing from bounding jumps. Javelin-throwing was as much as he would recommend and because winning the European title means so much to me I heeded his advice. Gold medals in the Olympic and Commonwealth Games have made me greedy for a set of three so that the championships in Stuttgart are my chief target, especially as I shall be meeting up with Felke and Lillak there, as well as Fatima. I love the Commonwealth Games like no other event but the gold in Edinburgh would be second-best for me.

I am giving serious consideration to retiring at the end of the season, unless ... well, there is a fair-sized 'unless'. Should my heels prove strong enough, I am determined to bid for the heptathlon. I have talked about this for five years now, speculating with Mary Peters and Daley Thompson on my maximums in the seven disciplines. I have to stop dreaming some time and put into practice my belief that, as I am far more powerful than when I broke the British record, I would score top marks in the throws in almost any company. The sprints and bounds which already feature in my regular training would stand me in good stead for all but the high-jump and 800 metres. I could hang in there in the latter for two laps which leaves the high-jump to make a fool of me. My bottom seems to weigh a ton and I can't heave it over the bar. Incidentally, I always declare my bottom when I am asked at customs if I have any identifying marks. I have a scar there from the time I tried to run away from my Dad and got my knickers stuck on a nail. I escaped with my knickers left hanging on a fence and a cut on my backside. So far no customs officer has asked for evidence! With the doctor's go-ahead, I would train through 1987 and compete at the Seoul Olympics the year after, always provided I was selected. Daley has already invited me to work with him and as Mary has promised her help, who better could I have as advisers than the double Olympic decathlon champion and the Munich pentathlon gold medallist? I wouldn't dare fail.

Seoul would definitely be my last competition, unless ... here we go again. If the Birmingham bid to host the 1992 Games should be successful then I could just be tempted to hang around until the ripe old age of 35 years old. This would bring me to my fifth Olympic Games and I feel tired just thinking about that. However, a British Games would be so historic – and unlikely to be repeated in our lifetimes – that the mere idea of competing gives me a thrill of anticipation. I share Ron Pickering's view that an Olympic Games here would give the nation a chance of establishing a new sense of identity and togetherness, not to mention patriotism. We are great belittlers of ourselves and, true to form, the opinion-makers in London initially greeted Birmingham's efforts with amused condescension. Britain is well on the way to becoming a two-nation state, north and south, and I hope it falls to my part of the country, the heart, to start healing the breach. I am delighted to be associated with the bid from a city where three times I have been voted West Midland Sports Personality of the Year. People there, indeed people all over the country, have kept faith with many a competitor through bad times and long after the London Press have written us off as has-beens. Many newspapermen stand us up for the joy of knocking us down, or so it seems. This is inexplicable to me. I am all in favour of rational criticism but not of confidence assassination. Some of the things written about me after Moscow set me crying all over again, reliving what were the worst moments of my life. It was during the first of these bouts of self-pity that Gary Newbon of Central Television put his arm around my shoulder and reminded me of Los Angeles four years in the future. Two years further on I am about to become involved, thanks to Gary and Central, in my first television series, a sports quiz called *Sporting Triangles*. So if you catch me with my head in a book this summer you will know I'm swotting up a few answers.

Which brings me to the present and future. Few jobs I have undertaken have compared with my workaday week as a Midlands promotion officer for the Duke of Edinburgh awards scheme. It has opened a window on another world for me, as it does for the 14- to 25-year olds who attempt to win medals by impressing in skill and service activities and an expedition or exploration. There is nothing more important today than taking young people off the streets and providing them with a challenge that will help them to build up self-respect, self-reliance and confidence. The expedition in particular does that: teenagers return home with a different attitude once they have fended for themselves in difficult or adventurous conditions. For a start, they discover they have a lot to learn, mainly about themselves. Around the schools I have had a tremendous response, especially from ethnic minority groups who tend to think that such schemes are not for them. They are precisely for them. It annoys me when kids of any colour say that they have lost heart because they are not accepted. I tell them they have to show that they are as good as anyone else and they will not do that by being shy and inhibited. I am stressing a similar message around Leeds where the city council have asked me to visit schools promoting sport and telling of some of my experiences.

I have been extremely lucky in my life because athletics has helped me achieve many of the targets I set myself when I was younger. I have won the most valued sports medal of all, I have travelled, I have met Muhammad Ali, I was even awarded a BSc by Wolverhampton Polytechnic and, through laughter and tears, God has protected me. There are dreams still – meeting Mother Teresa remains one of them.

Then I should like to marry and have a family: my children's names would be Chantelle for a girl because I have always loved the tinkling bells in the sound of it, maybe Daley for a boy because, well – even though I might give him a big head, he's the greatest athlete of them all. I would also like to coach for the WAAA and maybe to help with team management, for experience as a top-class competitor is always invaluable when dealing with girls of such determined character as athletes. But the greatest ambition of my life now is to return to the West Indies and to set up a giant athletics coaching school, attracting to it girls and boys whose talent would otherwise run to waste. You might think I am ungrateful and I can only reply by emphasising that I would hate to leave dear old England where there has always been someone with the faith in me to push me towards the heavens. And that is the point. In the Caribbean islands, there are far too few people pushing the thousands of kids who are pleading for a chance. I could have been one of them.

Career Record

1970

Major competitions: 6 June, Wolverhampton (Staffs Schools Champs) – 1st Jnr JT (29.70), 2nd HJ (1.47). 10 July, Solihull (English Schools Champs) – 3rd Jnr JT (31.86).

Season's best marks: HJ – 1.47, LJ – 5.45w/ 5.08, JT – 31.86.

Notes: Among the big names at the English Schools that year were: Charlie Spedding (7th Snr 1500), Brian Hooper (1st Snr PV), Dave Ottley (5th Inter JT), Steve Ovett (1st Jnr 400), Andrea Lynch (1st Snr 100), Gladys Taylor (2nd Snr 200), Sharon Colyear (1st Inter 200), Donna Murray (3rd Inter 200), Chris Tranter (Benning) (4th Inter 800), Sonia Lannaman (1st Jnr 100), Mary Stewart (2nd Jnr 800), Chris Boxer (3rd Jnr 800). The 31.86 ranked Tessa 7th among UK Juniors that year but the windy 5.45 LJ was bettered by only one Junior that season.

1971

Major competitions: 20 March, Cosford (WAAA Intermediate Indoor Champs) – 5th LJ (5.36). 8 May, Oldbury (Midland Intermediate Pentathlon Champs) – 1st (3590; LJ–5.41w, 200–28.4w, 80H – 14.4, SP–8.16, HJ–1.56). 5 June, Birmingham (Midland Intermediate Champs) – 1st LJ (5.46), 1st JT (37.48). 3 July, Birmingham Univ (WAAA Intermediate Pentathlon Champs) – 3rd (3604; 4.94, 27.3, 14.1, 8.25, 1.57). 9 July, Crystal Palace (English Schools Champs) – 8th Inter LJ (5.31). 31 July, Wolverhampton (WAAA Intermediate Champs) – 1st JT (42.02 – champ best), 7th HJ (1.50).

Season's best marks: JH – 1.58 (indoors), LJ – 5.50 (indoors), JT – 42.02, Intermediate Pent – 3604.

Notes: Ranked as top Intermediate javelin-thrower of year (42.02 ranked Tessa 16th

among UK Seniors in 1971); 8th on Intermediate Pentathlon list and 9th on LJ list. Picked for LJ and not JT in English Schools (her best at that stage of season was 38.44; title won with 39.26). English Schools win was considered a surprise; she beat Anne Goodlad (40.62), who had previously topped rankings with 41.72.

1972

Major Competitions: 18 March, Cosford (WAAA Intermediate Indoor Champs) – 2nd eq HJ (1.60), 4th LJ (5.35). 21 May, Warley (Midland Intermediate Pentathlon Champs) – 1st (3382; 5.58w, 26.6, 13.0, 7.96, 1.51). 3 June, Birmingham (Midland Intermediate Champs) – 1st LJ (5.65w – champ best), 2nd JT (35.86). 24 June, Watford (WAAA Intermediate Champs) – 1st JT (42.04). 8 July, Washington, Co Durham (English Schools Champs) – 1st Inter JT (43.06).

Season's best marks: 100 – 12.3, 200 – 25.6, 400 – 57.3, 100H – 15.6, HJ – 1.61 (indoors), LJ – 5.65w/5.56 (indoors), SP – 9.92, JT – 43.06, Intermediate Pentathlon – 3382.

Notes: Beaten in Midland Intermediate javelin by Janeen Williams of Cannock (37.60), but Williams only 3rd in WAAA Intermediate javelin. English Schools win despite elbow trouble having restricted Tessa's javelin training; other future greats in action included Ottley (2nd Snr JT), Ovett (1st Inter 800) and Coe (13th Inter 3000). Ranked top Inter in JT, 2nd in Pent, 4th eq in LJ, 5th in 400, 5th eq in 100H; ranked 11th on Senior javelin list.

1973

Major competitions: 13 Jan, Cosford (Cosford Games) – 3rd HJ (1.69), 4th 400 (59.3; 58.3 ht on 12 Jan). 12 May, Wolverhampton (Midland Pentathlon Champs) – 2nd (3453; 100H–15.5, SP–9.36, HJ–1.57, LJ–5.40, 200–27.6). 27 May, Warley (WAAA Pen-

177

tathlon Champs) – 5th (3639; 15.1, 8.77, 1.64, 5.53, 26.5). 2 June, Warley (Midland Champs) – 2nd JT (43.30). 6 July, Bebington (English Schools Champs) – 1st Snr JT (48.26). 20 July, Crystal Palace (WAAA Champs) – 7th JT (45.84; 48.36 qual). 25 Aug, Duisburg (European Junior Champs) – 12th JT (39.18). 19 Sept, Warley (UK v Sweden Juniors) – 2nd JT (48.46). 29 Sept, Crystal Palace (Inter-Area Pentathlon) – 7th (3732; 15.0w, 9.52, 1.64, 5.73, 26.7). 6 Oct, Crystal Palace (England Commonwealth Games Trials) – 1st JT (51.34; UK age–17 best).

Season's best marks: 400 – 58.2, 100H – 15.0w/15.1, HJ – 1.69, LJ – 5.75, SP – 11.01 (indoors), JT – 51.34, Pent – 3732.

Notes: At Cosford Games the 400 was won by Verona Bernard (Elder) in 55.3 and HJ by Barbara Inkpen (Lawton) whose 1.80 equalled the UK indoor best; Tessa duplicated that 1.69 outdoors, at Harlow on 6 June, and that remains her pb. Tom McNab, reporting on an indoor pentathlon at Cosford on 27 Jan (Tessa 4th with 3530), wrote: 'The best athlete pound for pound was undoubtedly Theresa Sanderson, a power-packed little athlete who could well high-jump 1.75 this year'. Winner of WAAA pentathlon was Mary Peters (4429). Winner of Midland javelin was Sharon Corbett (49.16), who also won WAAA title (53.88). Tessa added nearly 3m to her best when winning English Schools (48.26), and improved to 48.36 in WAAA qualifying round. She was well below form in European Junior but was throwing an unfamiliar model javelin; winner was Khristova of Bulgaria (54.84). Tessa upped pb to 48.46 in junior match v Sweden and 51.34 in Commonwealth Games Trials; she produced the winner in 4th round to overtake Sharon Corbett and Pru French, both of whom were over 50m in 1st round. Ranked 3rd on UK javelin list for year, 8th at pentathlon.

Tessa competed against Mary Peters in the 1973 WAAA Pentathlon at Warley: Mary won with 4429, Tessa was 5th with 3639.

1974

Major competitions: 29 Jan, Christchurch (Commonwealth Games) – 5th JT (48.54). 26 May, Crystal Palace (WAAA Pentathlon Champs) – 7th (3877; 14.9, 10.21, 1.68, 5.55, 25.6). 1 June, Warley (Midland Champs) – 1st JT (52.36; UK Junior rec). 9 June,

Bucharest (Romania v UK v FRG v Italy) – 5th JT (51.44). 19 June, Crystal Palace (UK v GDR) – 3rd JT (51.22). 29 June, Warsaw (Poland v UK v Canada) – 2nd JT (53.70; UK Jnr rec). 20 July, Crystal Palace (WAAA Champs) – 3rd JT (51.18). 27 July, Edinburgh (UK v Czechoslovakia v Netherlands) – 3rd JT (50.18). 31 July, Stockholm (Sweden v UK) – 1st JT (54.10; UK Jnr rec). 2 Sept, Rome (European Champs) – non-qualifier (13th; 53.28). 14 Sept, Warley (UK v FRG Juniors) – 1st JT (52.50). 21 Sept, Crystal Palace (British Women's Club Cup) – 1st JT (54.10; eq UK Jnr rec). 26 Sept, Crystal Palace (UK v Finland) 2nd (55.04; UK Jnr rec).

Season's best marks: 200 – 25.6, 100H – 14.9, HJ – 1.68, LJ – 5.69, SP – 10.21, JT – 55.04, Pent – 3877.

Notes: Cliff Temple reported in *Athletics World* on Commonwealth Games: 'Tessa was unlucky in that four of her throws were ruled fouls including several landing flat which might otherwise have given her a medal'. Petra Rivers (Aus) won with 55.48 ahead of Jenny Symon (Aus) 52.14, Sharon Corbett (Eng) 50.26 and Pru French (Eng) 50.00. Tessa's first full UK international was in Bucharest on 9 June; 10 days later she encountered the great Ruth Fuchs for the first time – Fuchs threw 65.58, Tessa 51.22. Qualified for European Champs (standard was 54m) when throwing 54.10 in Stockholm. At the Champs in Rome she was the best of the non-qualifiers and close to her best with 53.28 (top 12 got through); Fuchs won final with world record 67.22). Moved to 2nd on UK all-time list with 55.04 at end of season (Sue Platt's UK record stood at 55.60). Top ranked in UK for 1974, 9th in pentathlon.

1975

Major competitions: 10 May, Warley (Midland Pentathlon Champs) – 1st (3521; 15.8, 11.13, 1.50, 5.48, 27.1). 7 June, Warley (Midland Champs) – 1st JT (53.76). 21 June, Dresden (GDR v UK v Romania) – 4th JT (50.08). 12 July, Sofia (European Cup Semi) – 3rd JT (52.70). 19 July, Crystal Palace (WAAA Champs) – 1st (54.40). 16 Aug, Nice (European Cup Final) – 7th (48.72). 25 Aug, Crystal Palace (UK v USSR) – 2nd (52.88). 14 Sept, Edinburgh (UK v Sweden) – 1st (51.68).

Season's best marks: 100H – 14.4, 400H – 65.9, HJ – 1.62m LJ – 5.48, SP – 11.15, JT – 54.40, Pent – 3521.

Notes: First year she didn't improve in javelin but 54.40 still ranked her No 1 in UK. Encountered Ruth Fuchs three times: the East German threw 61.48 in Dresden, 63.20 in Sofia and 64.80 in Nice.

1976

Major competitions: 1 May, Split (Yugoslavia v UK v GDR) – 3rd JT (55.02). 8 May, Grangemouth (UK v Netherlands) – 1st JT (54.96). 22 May, Kiev (USSR v UK) – 4th JT (55.52). 11 June, Crystal Palace (Olympic Trials) – 1st JT (56.14; UK rec). 3 July, Crystal Palace (UK v Canada v Poland) – 3rd JT (55.74). 23 July, Montreal (Olympic qualifying round) – 7th JT (57.18; UK rec). 24 July, Montreal (Olympic final) – 10th JT (57.00). 21 Aug, Crystal Palace (WAAA Champs) – 1st JT (56.98). 30 Aug, Crystal Palace (British International Games) – 1st JT (57.20; UK rec).

Season's best marks: 100H – 14.1w/14.5, LJ – 5.54, SP – 11.98 (indoors), JT – 57.20.

Notes: Broke Sue Platt's UK record of 55.60 set in 1968 with 56.14 in Olympic Trials: 'It was a tremendous barrier for me'. Revised targets for year were to reach Olympic final and throw 60m. Broke UK record again in Olympic qualifying round (round 2 after first throw ruled flat). Produced her 2nd longest throw of 57.00 for 10th in Olympic final, won by Ruth Fuchs (GDR) with 65.94. At 20 she was the youngest finalist. Broke UK record for third time with 57.20 at Crystal Palace in a domestic competition.

1977

Major competitions: 29 Jan, Cosford (WAAA Indoor Champs) – 3rd 60H (8.6). 19 Feb, Dortmund (FRG v UK Indoors) – 4th 60H (9.03/8.76). 26 Feb, Cosford (UK v France Indoors) – 2nd 60H (8.5). 8 May, Wolverhampton (WAAA Pentathlon Champs) – 6th (3832; 14.2, 11.50, 1.63, 5.80, 2:39.3). 4 June, Warley (Midland Champs) – 1st JT (58.90; UK record) and 1st 400H (61.9). 11 June, Cwmbran (UK Champs) – 3rd 400H (60.46). 12 June, Cwmbran (UK Champs) – 1st JT (60.24; UK record). 22 June, Cologne – 6th JT (56.58). 25 June, Crystal Palace (Debenhams Jubilee Games) – 1st JT (57.76). 1 July, Dusseldorf – 1st JT (64.42; Commonwealth and UK rec). 10 July, Oulu (Finland v UK) – 1st JT (60.84). 17 July, Dublin (European Cup Semi-final) – 1st JT (67.20; Commonwealth and UK record). 26 July, Stockholm (Sweden v UK v Poland) – 1st JT (62.54). 7 Aug, Warley (GRE Cup Semi-final) – 1st JT (61.14). 13

Aug, Helsinki (European Cup Final) – 2nd JT (62.36). 20 Aug, Crystal Palace (WAAA Champs) – 1st JT (59.96), 3rd 100H (13.93). 26 Aug, Edinburgh (UK v USSR) – 1st JT (61.82). 2 Sept, Dusseldorf (World Cup) – 3rd JT (60.30). 9 Sept, Crystal Palace (Coca-Cola Meeting) – 1st JT (61.30). 11 Sept, Furth – 2nd JT (55.74). 17 Sept, Cwmbran (GRE Cup Final) – 1st JT (60.58).

Season's best marks: 100H – 13.93, 400H – 60.46, LJ – 5.80, SP – 11.50, JT – 67.20, Pent – 3832.

Notes: The year in which Tessa improved exactly 10 metres to rank second on the world all-time list; her versatility was such that she ranked 6th in UK at 100 and 400 hurdles and 10th in the new-style pentathlon (800m instead of 200m). Had her first meeting with young Fatima Whitbread at Crystal Palace on 25 June: Tessa won with 57.76; Fatima was 7th with 42.88. Defeated Olympic medallists Kate Schmidt (USA) and Marion Becker (FRG) when setting her first Commonwealth record of 64.42 in Dusseldorf. Greatest triumph of career (until LA Olympics) occurred in Dublin in European Cup semi when she became the first athlete in several years to beat Ruth Fuchs: 67.20 (Commonwealth record) to 64.46. Fuchs beat her, though, in European Cup Final: 68.92 to 62.36. Represented Europe in inaugural World Cup: 3rd (60.30) to Ruth Fuchs (62.36) and Nadyezhda Yakubovich (USSR) (62.02). Tessa voted Woman Athlete of the Year.

1978

Major competitions: 24 May, Crystal Palace (Philips Night of Athletics) – 1st JT (61.14). 11 June, Crystal Palace (UK v GDR) – 2nd JT (60.68). 17 June, Birmingham (Commonwealth Games Trials) – 1st JT (61.60). 24 June, Strasbourg (France v UK) – 1st JT (63.80). 2 July, Crystal Palace (UK v Bulgaria) – 1st JT (64.00). 9 July, Gateshead – 1st JT (60.64). 16 July, Edinburgh (UK Champs) – 1st JT (59.52). 10 Aug, Edmonton (Commonwealth Games) – 1st JT (61.34). 23 Aug, Crystal Palace (Rotary Watches Games) – 1st JT (62.98). 1 Sept, Prague (European Champs) – 2nd JT (62.40). 10 Sept, Crystal Palace (UK v Finland) – 1st JT (61.58). 15 Sept, Crystal Palace (Coca-Cola Meeting) – 1st JT (63.24). 25 Sept, Tokyo (Eight Nations) – 1st JT (62.66).

Season's best marks: 100H – 15.0, 400H – 63.2, LJ – 5.59w, JT – 64.00.

1979

Major competitions: 2 June, Bucharest – 1st JT (64.82). 10 June, Furth – 1st JT (65.34). 24 June, Bremen (FRG v UK v Poland v Switzerland) – 4th JT (58.72). 1 July, Cwmbran (European Cup Semi-final) – 1st JT (62.26). 28 July, Crystal Palace (WAAA Champs) – 1st JT (61.82). 4 Aug, Turin (European Cup Final) – 3rd JT (62.38). 14 Sept, Crystal Palace (Coca-Cola Meeting) – 1st JT (63.78). 23 Sept, Crystal Palace (UK v USSR) – 1st JT (64.04).

Season's best mark: JT – 65.34.

1980

Major competitions: 17 Jan, Melbourne – 1st JT (60.80). 22 Jan, Hobart – 1st JT (64.90). 25 Jan, Adelaide – 1st JT (60.80). 26 May, Cwmbran – 1st JT (64.02). 28 May, E Berlin – 2nd JT (62.62). 5 June, Stuttgart (FRG v UK v Romania) – 1st JT (69.70); Commonwealth rec). 27 June, Crystal Palace (Talbot Games) – 1st JT (64.38). 11 July, Stuttgart – 3rd JT (54.34). 13 July, (Amoco Games) – 2nd JT (61.88). 24 July, Moscow (Olympic Games) – non-qualifier JT (48.76). 8 Aug, Crystal Palace (Coca-Cola Meeting) – 3rd JT (60.08). 16 Aug, Crystal Palace (WAAA Champs) – 1st JT (64.08).

Season's best mark: JT – 69.70.

1981

Major competitions: 24 Jan, Auckland – 1st JT (63.72). 28 Jan, Wellington – 1st JT (57.00). 1 Feb, Christchurch – 1st JT (61.56). 4 Feb, Melbourne – 2nd JT (62.66). 8 Feb, Sydney – 2nd JT (62.58). 2 May, Birmingham – 1st JT (65.32). 9-10 May, Birmingham (Midland Heptathlon Champs) – 2nd (5841; 100H – 14.3, SP – 11.81, HJ – 1.60, 200 – 25.0, LJ – 5.80, JT – 60.60, 800 – 2:26.8). 30 May, Furth – 1st JT (68.86). 13-14 June, Saskatoon (Canada v UK Heptathlon) – 1st (5906; Commonwealth rec – 13.76, 12.68, 1.69, 25.28w, 5.80w, 57.76, 2:34.75). 24 June, Crystal Palace (UK v FRG v Poland) – 1st JT (65.28). 5 July, Edinburgh (European Cup Semi-final) – 1st JT (65.04). 11-12 July, Brussels (European Heptathlon Cup Semi-final) – 2nd (6110; Commonwealth rec – 13.72, 12.78, 1.63, 24.89, 5.97, 64.64, 2:26.20). 25 July, Crystal Palace (WAAA Champs) – 2nd 100H (13.46), 13th LJ (5.89). 2 Aug, Spalding – 1st JT (67.24). 17 Aug, Zagreb (European Cup Final) – 2nd JT (65.94). 31 Aug, Crystal Palace (Amoco Games) – 1st JT (68.60). 11 Sept, Crystal Palace (Coca-Cola Meeting) – 1st JT (68.72). 13 Sept, Birmingham – 1st JT (65.96). 19 Sept, Birmingham (GRE Cup Final) – 1st JT (63.84).

Season's best marks: 200 – 24.89, 100H – 13.46, HJ – 1.69, LJ – 5.97, SP – 13.27, JT – 68.86, Hept – 6110.

1982

Major competitions: 30 Jan, Cosford (WAAA Indoor Champs) – 8th LJ (5.83). 28 Aug, Coatbridge (UK Women's League) – 1st JT (66.00).

Season's best marks: LJ – 5.83 (indoors), SP – 12.58, JT – 66.00.

1983

Major competitions: 17 Apr, Acoteias – 1st JT (64.08). 28 May, Edinburgh (UK Champs) – 2nd JT (61.44). 5 June, Birmingham (UK v USSR) – 1st JT (70.82; Commonwealth rec). 11 June, Maribor (Yugoslavia v England v Hungary) – 1st JT (65.42). 26 June, Edinburgh (Tarmac Edinburgh Games) – 1st JT (73.58; Commonwealth rec). 28 June, Oslo – 1st JT (64.88). 3 July, Spalding – 1st JT (64.20). 10 July, Birmingham (England v Scotland) – 1st JT (65.84). 12 Aug, Helsinki (World Champs) – qualified JT (64.80). 13 Aug, Helsinki (World Champs) – 4th JT (64.76).

Season's best mark: JT – 73.58.

1984

Major competitions: 16 May, Leeds – 1st JT (66.14). 20 May, Bolzane – 1st JT (68.58). 6 June, Crystal Palace (Olympic Trials) – 1st JT (67.02). 13 June, Florence – 1st JT (66.76). 19 June, Belfast – 1st JT (68.88). 23 June, Birmingham (England v Scotland v Wales v Yugoslavia) – 1st JT (62.52). 13 July, Crystal Palace (Peugeot Talbot Games) – 2nd JT (67.88). 15 July, Birmingham – 2nd JT (62.54). 21 July, Potsdam – 3rd JT (67.92). 5 Aug, Los Angeles (Olympic Games) – qualified JT (61.58). 6 Aug, Los Angeles (Olympic Games) 1st JT (69.56; Olympic rec).

PERSONAL BESTS

100 – 12.3 (1972), 200 – 24.89 (1981), 400 – 57.3 (1972), 800 – 2:26.20 (1981), 100H – 13.46 (1981), 400H – 60.46 (1977), HJ – 1.69 (1973 & 1981), LJ – 5.97 (1981), SP – 13.27 (1981), JT – 73.58 (1983), Hept – 6110 (1981).

Career Record

ANNUAL PROGRESSION (Javelin)

1970	31.86	1978	64.00
1971	42.02	1979	65.34
1972	43.06	1980	69.70
1973	51.34	1981	68.86
1974	55.04	1982	66.00
1975	54.40	1983	73.58
1976	57.20	1984	69.56
1977	67.20	1985	71.18

TESSA v FATIMA

1977 (2–0) 25 June: 57.76 – 42.88; 9 Sept: 61.30 – 46.48.

1978 (8–0) 24 May: 61.14 – 51.34; 11 June: 60.08 – 51.80; 17 June: 61.60 – 50.50; 24 June: 63.80 – 49.46; 2 July: 64.00 – 53.34; 16 July: 59.52 – 52.52; 10 Aug: 61.34 – 49.16; 10 Sept: 61.58 – 51.06.

1979 (5–0) 20 May: 62.04 – 46.16; 24 June: 58.72 – 56.34: 28 July: 61.82 – 56.66; 14 Sept: 63.78 – 48.48; 23 Sept: 64.04 – 54.60.

1980 (2–0) 8 Aug: 60.08 – 57.74; 16 Aug: 64.08 – 56.24.

1981 (1–0) 24 June: 65.28 – 64.18.

1983 (3–2) 28 May: 61.44 – 62.14; 5 June: 70.82 – 67.46; 26 June: 73.58 – 68.36; 28 June: 64.88 – 63.16; 13 Aug: 64.76 – 69.14.

1984 (1–2) 13 July: 67.88 – 67.96; 15 July: 62.54 – 67.16; 6 Aug: 69.56 – 67.14.

TESSA'S COMPETITIONS IN 1985

14 June, Madrid: 1st (71.18)

29 June, Gateshead: (UK v France V Czech) 2nd (64.32) (1, Whitbread 68.84)

7 July, Birmingham: (UK v GDR) 3rd (64.80) (1, Felke 72.82; 2, Whitbread 66.30)

14 July, Budapest: (Hungary v England) 1st (63.36)

20 July, Crystal Palace: 3rd (65.22 (1, Whitbread 68.32)

23 July, Edinburgh: 5th (59.38) (1, Whitbread 70.14)

26 July, Birmingham: (WAAA Champs) 1st (66.38)

9 Aug, Gateshead: 2nd (66.22) (1, Whitbread 68.08)

22 Aug, Espoo (Fin): 2nd (65.08) (1, Lillak 65.86)